No Poverty and Diakonia

No Poverty and Diakonia

Towards a Vision of Diakonia in Korea

Korean Diakonia

No Poverty and Diakonia
Towards a Vision of Diakonia in Korea

Copyright © Korean Diakonia
All rights reserved.

Publisher: Kim, Sam-whan
Editor: Cheon, Young-cheol

ISBN 13: 9791195960811

KD Publications
Seoul, South Korea
www.koreandiakonia.org

CONTENTS

Preface

Rev. Dr Kim, Sam-whan
President of Korean Diakonia

GOD IS LOVE (1 John 4:16). God loves us so much that S/He came down to the earth in His/Her human body. Jesus came to this world not to be served but to serve it up to his death on the cross (Mark 10:45). God called us as human beings to serve the Kingdom of God.

It is absolutely through the divine grace that the Republic of Korea has achieved astonishing development without precedent in the world history. God has used in His/Her significant way the works of the Korean Churches and Christians for this country today. All of our thanks should be attributed to God, and I pray that our Korean Churches will follow the way of *Diakonia* in a way more pertinent to its divine calling.

God wants to disclose the divine glory to this world by utilizing the grace and blessing we have been given (Matthew 5:16). There are still so many people in our society who desperately need our helping hands. There are also many people who have suffered from all kinds of disasters, diseases and wars around the world as well as in domestic areas. Our Korean Churches should come down to the places of Diakonia under very poor conditions and try to find a way to serve them by humbling ourselves like our Lord. We also will have to prepare works of Diakonia for the coming age of the unification of Korean peninsula, embracing in love the people of the North Korea. Just as God has given us all things we have freely, so we should give our neighbors what they need as freely. Just as God has overpoured our cups, so we should share more with this society.

In this 'Diakonia Korea Expo 2016,' many not-so-well-known works of Diakonia in the Korean churches were introduced to the public, and many of seminars and meetings were held to prepare for better works. I wish that this Expo be the place where we remembered the divine grace God has conferred upon us and glorified only God. I believe that this Expo was the place where we encouraged the people who have committed their lives to Diakonia works and support their works and sweat. I hope this Expo gave comport and support to our suffering neighbors. Most of all, I do really want this Expo to be the place where we decided to commit our lives to Our Lord's mission of Diakonia and sharing.

This book is a collection of presentation papers from Germany, Netherlands, Sweden, China and Cuba at the International Seminar on Diakonia during 'Diakonia Korea Expo 2016' whose main theme was "No Poverty and Diakonia." This also includes "Towards a Vision of Diakonia in Korea: the declaration of Diakonia Korea Expo 2016."

All glory should be given to God, and I bless in the name of our Lord all participants in Diakonia Korea Expo 2016.

Towards a Vision of Diakonia in Korea: The Declaration of Diakonia Korea Expo 2016

1. Introduction

In a period in which there was no gospel and freedom of faith in Korea, Diakonia paved the way to the introduction of the gospel in terms of medical and educational missions. Ever since then, the Korea Church has played the roles of light and salt for this society whenever this nation has suffered, for example, from Japanese Coercive Occupation, Korean War and the ever-increasing polarization of the wealth between the rich and the poor since the recent economic development and growth.

The Korean Church has felt a need to specialize and organize the works of Diakonia in response to the rapidly changing social demands in the 21ˢᵗ century. Responding to the need, 'Korea Christian Society Welfare' was established in 2002, and this organization initiated a momentum to build a Diakonia network over the country beyond the level of individual churches by holding 'Christian Social Welfare Expo 2005.' Korean Diakonia, which was launched in 2007, unified with 'Korea Christian Society Welfare' in 2009 and in turn with Hope Solidarity of Korea Church in 2010 and has become a representative organization of Diakonia organizations in Korea. Its contributions are as followings:

(1) Korean Diakonia has systematically organized the works of Christian social welfare and made Christian social welfare an academic discipline.

It published *The Comprehensive List of Christian Social Welfare in Korea* (2007) and performed surveys of the homeless (2009, 2012). It also held the Diakonia Academy of Korea Church to catalyze the solidarity of Diakonia organizations in Korean churches (2014). Korean Diakonia holds 'Christian Social Welfare Expo' every 5 years (2005, 2010).

    (2) Korean Diakonia has contributed to emergency relief works domestic and abroad.

Korean Diakonia organized 170,000 Christian volunteers in the Hebei Spirit's oil spill accident (2007), and it has also provided food relief to North Korea (2008), emergency relief to the victims of the cyclone disaster in Myanmar, to the victims of the earthquake in Sichuan Province, China (2008), to the flood victims in Philippines, to those of the earthquake in Indonesia (2009) and Haiti (2010), to the victims of the tsunami in Japan (2011), and to the refuges from Syria (2013). Further, Korean Diakonia supported the recovery of the damaged schools from the cyclone in Philippines and provided aids to Palestine, Gaza, and Jordan (2014). It also participated in the emergency relief for the victims of the earthquakes in Nepal (2015) and Ecuador (2016).

    (3) Korean Diakonia has suggested mediation in the matters of social conflicts and tried to resolve them.

Korean Diakonia suggested its mediation in the tragic disaster of YongSan redevelopment project (2009), provided the accommodations for the surviving comfort women (2010), and ran a consolation project for the victims of Sewol ferry disaster (2014).

Korean Diakonia here in Diakonia Korea Expo 2016, as the third Christian Social Welfare Expo, makes public the document, "Towards a Vision of Diakonia in Korea," and in so doing presents the orientation of Diakonia in the Korean Church.

2. SIGNS OF THE AGE

Our human civilization in the 20th century has experienced wars and genocides due to various reasons such as colonialism, the cold war, racial conflicts and so on. While the material foundation of the civilization has prospered well, the shadows of poverty, starvation, and exploitation have never retired, but they instead have kept coming back with the face of dehumanization. The destruction of the environment by selfish human greed has resulted in the ever-increasing frequency of natural disasters and the acceleration of the extinctions of various and precious natural species. The 21st century does not seem to promise us a better future, rather we just anticipate a worse reality in which the lives of the poor will be more difficult than in the 20th century. We Christians feel a great responsibility to be aware of the divine will among the signs of the age.

(1) The neo-liberal economic globalization has maximized the profits of the privileged few over the globe and driven all societies around the world into an arena of unlimited competition. Further, the modern materialism has misled us to a false belief that the creation and accumulation of wealth are the supreme norm for human society and the only solution to various human problems, distorting values and ethics for human spirituality. The gap between the rich and the poor has been ever increasing all over the globe, and, as the traditional units of community that have served as the protection for people and citizen, such as nation, region and family have collapsed, the quality of life for people who cannot secure their own happiness and security has deteriorated. The increasing number of immigrants and refugees over the globe is its result or symptom.

(2) There are two extreme tides in this age. There has been the strong current of secular atheism, on the one hand, and the continual increase of aggressive religious fanaticism, on the other hand. Although secularism has contributed to the de-superstition of religions, it also has played a key role in the commodification of the sacredness of life and the materialization of human relations. Religious fundamentalism based upon religious vision and identity has threatened, dominated, controlled and destroyed the peoples who do not submit to its oppressive power and agree to its identity. These

extremes of religious cultures do not provide any seed of hope for the vulnerable minority and the marginalized. They just make their lives worse than ever.

(3) Nations and communities have used violence and war as their means to get what they want without any satisfaction.

(4) There are millions of refugees and foreign laborers, who have fled from wars, violence, drought, famine, poverty, hunger, starvation and so on. The violation of human rights and the discrimination against them have radically increased and intensified. Moreover, economic anxiety with narrow-minded nationalism justifies and rationalizes "xenophobia" and racism.

(5) There have been dramatically increased violence and discrimination against racial and religious minorities, victims of social caste, women and children, handicapped people and elderly people.

(6) The global chain of life in creation has been destroyed due to the global climate change, the ecological crisis, and the exhaustion of nature. Natural disasters have been more frequent, partly due to the destruction of environments, and this in turn has raised the burden of poor people, especially in underdeveloped countries.

(7) The Korean society now has been suffering from the increasing rate of the unemployment of the young generation, the low birth rate, the surge of the aging population, the breakdown of family and a youth problem. It means that the blind spots of the social welfare system in our society have become ever enlarged and more in number.

These signs of this age just show that our Diakonia ministry of Korean churches in the 21st century has become a more urgent and important work than ever.

3. THE BIBLICAL AND THEOLOGICAL ORIENTATION OF DIAKONIA

The Hebrew, "abad," in the Bible basically means "to worship God," but, at the same time, it has another meaning, "to serve" or "service." It means that

Christian worship and service cannot be separated. Our service (diaconia) is nothing but the expression of our thanks to God's love and our practical response to the divine love. The Hebrew Bible gives the list of our neighbors Christians should serve as the poor, orphans, widows and strangers. God is the one who helps orphans (Psalm 10:14), who rescues the poor (Psalm 35:10), and who defends orphans and widows and loves the alien (Deut. 10:18; Psalm 146:9). God commanded Israelites to serve them (Isaiah 1:17, Deut. 24:17-21). What God wants is that there be no vulnerable and poor among His chosen nation, and thus God gave the chosen people the responsibility and duty of serving and helping each other. The servant of God has "to preach good news to the poor, to bind up the brokenhearted, to proclaim freedom for the captives and release from darkness for the prisoners" (Isaiah 61:1-2).

Jesus Christ came to serve human beings (Mark 10:45) and lived as a "servant" (Luke 22:27). For Jesus, the commandment "to love your neighbors as yourself" is the same as the first and greatest commandment to "love the Lord your God with all your heart and with all your soul and with all your mind" (Matthew 22:39). Jesus said to the lawyer, who was asking him the way to eternal life, "do this", by telling him the parable of the good Samaritan (Luke 10: 37). He said the young man who said he kept all the commandments, "go and sell all you possess and give to the poor, and … follow me"(Mark 10:21). Also by washing the feet of his disciples, Jesus showed that the identity of faith community lies in its serving (John 13:14). Jesus's healing ministry and his table community with sinners anticipatively showed the essence of the community in the kingdom of God. Diakonia is nothing but the way of discipleship, and it has to do with the measures of the Last Judgment (Matthew 25:31-46). By telling them, 'take up one's own cross and follow me,' Jesus wants disciples to express their discipleship under the cross (Matthew 16:24).

St Paul understood Diakonia as the fulfillment of the law (Rome 13:8). He acknowledged that Diakonia cannot bring salvation, but that it can be a proof for judgment (1 Cor. 3:13; 2 Cor. 5:10). Diakonia is the mission of serving, and it witnesses that the grace of God in Christ is expensive and precious.

The authenticity of our faith will be decided upon whether or not one practices love (James 2:17).

Piety before God cannot be separated from Diakonia, especially in the Old Testament and the early Christian Church.

> *Pure and undefiled religion in the sight of our God and Father is this: to visit orphans and widows in their distress, and to keep oneself unstained by the world*

> (JAMES 1: 27).

In face of the 500th anniversary of the Reformation, we reaffirm that Diakonia is the essential mission of the Church and the fruit of the gospel, realizing that it recovers the importance of the precious divine grace and that it plays its pivotal role in the ecumenical movement and reformation of our churches.

(1) Diakonia is the essential mission of the Church

The Church, which is called and guided by the Holy Spirit through baptism, participates in the *Missio Dei* (the mission of God) through Diakonia. Diakonia is an important way to express the divine love which discloses itself in Jesus Christ. Also, it anticipatively shows that the Kingdom of God, which is fulfilled through the gospel, is none other than a community of love. For the essence of the kingdom of God lies in our serving and loving, not in our dominating and subjugating. Thus, the Church should not remain as an exclusive or introverted community of faith, but it should manifest itself as the light and salt of the world by witnessing to the gospel and serving the others in love. Diakonia is the essential mission of the Church as well as the mission of all Christians. It means that each Christian should not content oneself with donating some money to special organizations of Diakonia as the fulfillment of one's responsibility of serving and sharing.

(2) Diakonia is the fruit of justification through faith in the divine grace.

"The ax is already at the root of the trees, and every tree that does not produce good fruit will be cut down and thrown into the fire" (Matthew 3:10). As a tree without fruits is useless, churches and Christians without their mission of Diakonia make the grace of Christ "cheap grace." Diakonia is costly discipleship, and it rejects cheap grace, which lacks the love of our neighbors, and prosperity theology, which lacks the meaning of sacrifice.

(3) Diakonia is an 'element of worship' and thus 'worship after worship.'

The love of God and the love of neighbors must go together in worship, and this lies in the core of true Christian piety (James 1:27). God does not accept any worship without Diakonia (Micah 6:8). For the reformers, the office of Diakonia was a necessary element for piety before and after worship. When the Korean Church abuses Diakonia as one of the programs for church growth, it is none other than disloyalty to Jesus's commandment to love one's neighbors as oneself. Diakonia should be accompanied with authenticity and piety together.

(4) Diakonia is a way of participating in the divine mission, in which God first works at marginalized areas.

Jesus proclaimed the Gospel of the Kingdom of God in Nazareth, Galilee. His mission had its priority for the small and the lost. However, we read, "Can anything good come from [Nazareth]?" (John 1:46). God works for and among the marginalized, and thus the center of our mission work has to be marginalized areas.

Thus, Diakonia now should be understood from the perspective of people in marginalized communities, not from the perspective of providers. Diakonia should not be an expression of paternalism, which is content with wrapping a bandage around the wound of the victim(s). Diakonia must be carried out until it will fixes the root cause of the wound and the pain.

(5) Diakonia recovers the ecumenism of the Church and plays its key role in church reformation.

Diakonia is an element to unite divided churches. To recover Koinonia (friendship) between the Jerusalem church and the churches of the aliens, St Paul collected donations from the churches of the aliens and paid a visit to the church of Jerusalem, risking his life. "For if the Gentiles have shared in the Jews' spiritual blessings, they owe it to the Jews to share with them their material blessings" (Rome 15:27). As the Reformation in the 16th century recovered the essence of Christian faith through the Bible, grace and belief, our reformation in the 21ˢᵗ century should show the power of the gospel in recovering the discipleship of Diakonia.

4. Challenges and Tasks

In 2015, the United Nations (UN) announced "Sustainable Development Goals" (SDGs). The agenda consist of 17 goals, and it presents an orientation under which the world community should go forward together in its awareness of the basic situations of poverty and environment.[1] This agenda urges the establishment of solidarity within the frames of world solidarity and the environment on the earth, and it also asks the Korea Church to participate in fulfilling the same goals. In face of these challenges and tasks, our Korea Church with its Christian conscience and moral responsibility for the world presents our vision of Diakonia as followings:

> (1) Diakonia of the Korean Church is to recover and protect the dignity of the image of God in all human beings.

All human beings have their own dignity, and they are all equal before God. God's love is to do justice for the weak, to actualize equality based on justice in community, and to achieve dignity for all forms of life. In this context, the deficiency model cannot be a right model of welfare which categorizes the socially weak as the target of welfare and understands its task as to fill the deficiency and loss. This deficiency model separates the subject from the object and alienates the weak. Diakonia sees provider and beneficiaries together as companions, and it leads them to the establishment of a healthy community.

---

1 The 17 goals are as followings: (1) no poverty, (2) zero hunger, (3) good health and well-being, (4) quality education, (5) gender equality, (6) clean water and sanitation, (7) affordable and clean energy, (8) decent work and economic growth, (9) industry, innovation and infrastructure, (10) reduced inequalities, (11) sustainable cities and communities, (12) responsible consumption and production, (13) climate action, (14) life below water, (15) life on land, (16) peace, justice and strong institutions, and (17) partnerships for the goals.

(2) The Diakonia of the Korean Church is to be a contribution to the common good for the society.

Diakonia must go beyond the perspective of provider, in which the world becomes the 'other' to receive our service. Our church needs to overcome a temptation to use the works of Diakonia for the expansion of the church that comes from a selfish motivation. Rather it needs to focus on its mission to deliver Christian value to the world. The Korean Church should believe in the cosmic sovereignty of God and take up its service for the Common Good, understanding itself as part of social and global communities. In order to do so, the Korean Church should extend its solidarity of Diakonia over the government and civil society, and further over the global villages. All churches and faith communities should share the awareness of Diakonia through active discussions and responses.

(3) The Korean Church should be the subject to serve local societies through its volunteer works.

The foundation of the Korean Church is local churches. There are various areas such as local governments, local administrations, diverse organizations of welfare, non-profit organizations and civil organizations, and they are waiting for the participation of churches in their works. There are also the blind spots of welfare in local societies. Caring for those on the second-to-the-bottom economic level, emergency welfare aid and volunteer work all are the areas only churches can take up. The most serious matter faced by the contemporary society is the collapse of family. Churches can serve local societies by providing educational programs for family and caring for disintegrating families.

The Korean Church is the biggest resource for volunteer work. Human resources with their commitment and the organized force of churches can be the most valuable ones for local societies. Volunteered Christians can have a chance to see this social structure through the eyes of faith. Diakonia of the Korean Church should not be left as the works of professionals. It should seek for a chance to become a channel for Christians to participate in civil society and for the society to come one step closer to the Church.

(4) Diakonia of the Korean Church should prepare for the coming age of unification.

Although South and North Koreas are divided now, Korean Christians believe that the grace of God will realize the unification of these divided nations. As seen in the case of Germany, unification is not just about political unification but also about social unification. North Korea is under the condition of absolute poverty. It is not possible for this society to recover and restore human dignity and value without unconditional support from South Korea. Without this support as well as collaboration by the South, unification may turn into catastrophe, instead of blessing, for the two societies.

Thus, Diakonia of the Korean Church should prepare for the coming age of unification. It is not just about economic assistance, but it also includes a responsible role in achieving social integrity with new value, new worldview and spiritual life. Given the politically fierce conflict between the North and the South, the states cannot take on this pivotal role for the unification alone. The Church should cultivate its capability for attaining social integrity by reforming a model of society through education and service.

(5) The Korea Church should pave the way to Diakonia for the global age.

Korea has had a unique experience of growth from an aid-receiving country to an aid-giving country. In this context, Korea has been asked for a leadership in international politics, and it is time for Korea to take its responsibility, pertinent to its international status, for underdeveloped countries over the world. Thus, South Korea needs discernment and practice to contribute to the global welfare of human civilization as well as its national welfare.

This requires that Koreans have a responsible attitude towards immigrant foreigners in domestic areas. Given the reality of globalization within this society, Koreans really needs a mature attitude to give up their exclusive and alienating mind and to try to embrace and co-exist with different cultures and ethnicities.

The Korean Church benefited very much from the aids of the world church in the past. It also had a privileged experience of globalization through its international exchange and mission works with the world church. Are all these "for such a time as this?" (Esther 4:14). The Korean Church has a responsibility to widen the horizon of Diakonia for an age of globalization.

(6) Diakonia of the Korean Church should be a work to make life abundant.

Under the neo-liberal economy system based upon the principle of the survival of the fittest and the law of the jungle, unlimited competition has driven to the verge of extinction all forms of life on the earth as well as the traditional structures of nation, region and family. Following Jesus who came to the earth in order to give abundant life, the Korea Church should seek for Diakonia which revives and prospers life abundantly.

Diakonia, which revives life, has to struggle against absolute poverty. The United Nations has worked for its Millennium Goal to end world poverty. As a result, the state of absolute poverty has been decreased to half, and the world now can have a hope to eliminate absolute poverty with its communal effort.

The Korean Church in its cooperation with various social and civil organizations should provide a hope to solve the matters of the extreme economic polarization of our society and its relative poverty. Social concern for people from diverse classes who dropped out after bloody competition is absolutely needed now. The right value of life should be shared with the so-called losers such as the young generation, who have been suffering from the high rate of unemployment, women who suffer from the low rate of employment and the status of underemployment, and the elderly who live under poverty and alienation. Most of all, a safety net of our society should be provided to those who live under the condition of absolute poverty.

5. PROPOSALS

For the growth of the Diakonia calling of the Korean Church, we propose some practical tasks as follows:

(1) Diakonia affirms that the Korean Church has a social mission to recover social trust, respect and acknowledgment.

(2) The Church should seek for a coherence of their services to construct a Diakonia network among churches for more specialized services beyond an individual church-centered or denomination-centered approach.

(3) It is not the spirit of Jesus Christ to force a confession of faith from the weak in need as a medium of material aid. The Church should practice the love of Christ as it is, and it should pray that the love of Christ bear its fruits in its mission.

(4) The Church needs help from professionals to check out what kinds of help local societies need and has the responsibility to realize it with its effective and sustainable serving.

(5) The Church puts its primary concern onto those who are excluded from the social welfare system of the state, thus those who are left at the blind sports of welfare and those who are need of better care.

(6) Diakonia must not have any discrimination based upon nationality, language, ideology, culture and origin. All human beings have right to be served as equal persons with the image of God. Emergency relief should be preferentially given to places where famine, starvation, or earthquake occurs.

(7) Diakonia should have its priority to rescue the lives of children under starvation and/or malnutrition, especially in the areas of North Korea and Africa.

(8) With regard to humanitarian aid, the Church has to cooperate with governments and non-government organizations (NGOs) specialized in relief works.

(9) The Church should accept and develop a theology of Diakonia and do its best to include the Diakonia field in the curriculum of theological education.

Diakonia against Poverty

Henry von Bose
Evangelical Mission in Solidarity, Germany

1. The Social Welfare Service of Protestant Churches in Wuerttemberg

All of Diakonia's work is based in the Protestant conviction. We strive to fashion ourselves after God's unconditional love as embodied by Jesus Christ. Diakonia addresses the wants and needs of others based on the Christian view of mankind. This view includes the belief that every human being is vulnerable, and needs love and forgiveness. Some are in greater need of help than others. Diakonia carries out its mission to practise charity in the model of Jesus Christ by offering a wide range of support, including practical aid and legal representation.

The services of Diakonia typically offer their assistance in the proximity of residential areas. This means that Diakonia is present all over our country Wuerttemberg in the south-western part of Germany. The way the Diakonia network is set up ensures that cooperation with the different services and service units of Diakonia in Wuerttemberg is close and excellent.

More than 40,000 are employed within Diakonia in Wuerttemberg, they do their work in more than 2,000 services and social work units. Another 30,000 voluntary workers are committed to activities within Diakonia. The Social Welfare Service of the Protestant Churches is the umbrella association gathering all the social service institutions and entities that exist within the Protestant Churches in Wuerttemberg. The Baptist and Methodist Churches belong to them also. The Service is charged with four decisive tasks to fulfill:

It represents all of the church's social work. Thus, its responsibility includes supporting church communities with the implementation of their diaconal mission and tasks.

Representing all of its members, it serves the members' diaconal work and service units. More so, it serves as a converging or focal point for the members' interests and services and represents these when addressing German politics or the Church as such.

As a welfare service agency, it is partner vis-à-vis the German government and is consulted on issues pertaining to the requirements and needs of the German welfare state. As an organization following Jesus' teachings, it serves as an advocate on behalf of people in need and of the underprivileged in politics and society, especially those who are being discriminated against. It is committed to fighting societal causes of poverty and discrimination and strives and works for more social justice.

Altogether, Diakonia in Wuerttemberg looks after and supports more than 270,000 people, many of them live in homes run by a Diakonia service unit. Diakonia is active in the fields of work as follows: welfare for handicapped people; care for the sick; care for old people; support for the unemployed, for the homeless, for the heavily indebted, and for other poor people in society; support for drug addicts and those at risk; support for migrants, refugees and asylum-seekers, especially when discriminated against; support for girls and women in distress.

In-patient service units, out-patient units, as well as day services and individual care for persons - all that is within the range of offerings provided by Diakonia.

Diakonia creates jobs on the market that is sponsored by the government. The "employment companies" of Diakonia belong to the sector of publicly subsided work. They try to qualify unemployed people and to empower them in cooperation with private industry for a change into regular employment.

They also improve the occupational integration of the long-term unemployed. Also, Diakonia provides special shopping centers for the poor.

Diakonia runs schools and job training for young people. In earlier years when we had conscription in Germany, Diakonia offered placement for conscientious objectors. They had the chance to do civil service instead of military service for a legally prescribed time.

Nowadays a lot of young people spend a voluntary social year after finishing school as a service to the society and an orientation in finding out the best choice of a profession for themselves.

A wide range of voluntary service done by people of all ages is a kind of quality label of Diakonia.

Volunteers are informed and attracted by advertising in the congregations and diaconal services. They get an introduction to the service, they will work at. They are rewarded with personal liability and accident insurance, reimbursement of expenses (costs of traveling from home to the place of voluntary employment and back home) and further training programmes, they participate in regular meetings with colleagues and professional companions. The volunteer's social service contains great potential for creativity and is welcome as a completion of the professionals. They make a contribution of high value to the social culture in the society.

INTERNATIONAL TASKS

The Diakonia in Wuerttemberg is a member of The Protestant Agency for Diakonia and Development of Germany's Protestant churches. The agency carries out the church's mission through its aid programmes "Bread for the World" - Protestant Development Service and "Emergency Aid". "Emergency Aid" provides emergency services and disaster relief in crisis situations worldwide. "Bread for the World", the development and relief agency, supports long-term development projects and empowers the poor and marginalized to improve their living conditions in more than 90 countries all across the globe. An essential feature of the projects is the close and continuous cooperation with local, often church-related partner organizations. Upon request, "Bread for the world" provides them with specialists and volunteers. " Bread for the World" is member of ACT Alliance, "Action by Churches Together", one of the biggest alliances for emergency relief and development help worldwide. Every year the offerings of all protestant congregations in Germany at Christmas time are dedicated to "Bread for the World" about 60 Million Euro are collected yearly.

MEANS OF FINANCING

Own resources and Social Security Funds: Diakonia delivers many forms of assistance which the people needing help pay for themselves. German Social Security assumes a part of these expenses and thus take some of the burden off those who need assistance. For instance, intensive care in an old people's home, or at the old person's home, is being assumed in part by the health care insurance mandatory in Germany. Our Social Security helps finance the rehabilitation measures and rehabilitation hospitals run by Diakonia. The German Federal Employment Office supports the Diakonia service assisting unemployed people.

Subsides from Public Funds: Part of the expenses are being supported from public funds (federal, state and municipal level). For example, the state pays for a part of the costs occurring in treating drug or alcohol addicts or for women struggling with pregnancy (regarding abortion). Or, the municipalities pay for integration services for handicapped and give additional funds benefitting mentally, or psychologically ill people or those heavily indebted.

Church Tax: Every member of the Protestant Church in Germany has to pay a church tax (collected in lieu by the German Internal Revenue Service). This tax is levied according to the member's income and/or salary. The majority of consultancy services and contact points of diaconal district services are being funded by this church tax. Child day care centers receive supplementary funds. Furthermore, assistance for immigrants from former Soviet Unions, for foreigners and for refugees are being financed.

Donations: This kind of financial means is becoming increasingly important. Thanks to donations, Diakonia is able to help those who do not have a rightful claim for help and for whom nobody feels responsible. Poor people get meals at low costs in the so-called "Vesperkirchen" - food churches - and they get free medical aid. Or they can buy food at very low prices in special shops. Families with handicapped children also get help in a non-bureaucratic way. Without such donations it would not be possible to assist people after catastrophes in Germany and abroad.

2. MERCY AND JUSTICE

So far, this is a glance over Diakonia in my country as it is constituted today after a long development. Please, let me have a look back. When I came to South Korea for the first time in 1994, we were invited by PCK to discuss questions concerning social responsibility of the Church. How is Diakonia established within the Bible and what is the meaning of Diakonia for life and organization of a congregation? Which structures does the social commitment of the Church necessitate?

These were questions that our churches in Germany and Europe were dealing with at that time as well. In 1996 we came for the second time and were guests at the inauguration of the Institute of Diakonia Science at Hanil University & Presbyterian Theological Seminary. With us, we brought a declaration that had been issued by the Conference of European Churches in Bratislava, the capital of Slovakia, in 1994: "Towards a Vision of Diakonia in Europe." Thus, our Korean friends were included in a vast ecumenical movement: It was our goal to cement the standing of Diakonia in the Church. Let me quote a sentence from the Bratislava Declaration: "Diakonia is an extension of worship into everyday life." The proclamation and celebration of faith on Sunday has an impact on the everyday life of church members. During the week, the hearers of the Word authenticate the Gospel and thus become doers of the Word. This takes place by love. They say "Amen" to the Gospel they have heard proclaimed and ask for the power of the Holy Spirit. He helps them to live as disciples of our Lord Jesus Christ. Paul writes to the Galatians (5:6): "Faith expresses itself through love." Faith gives energy to love. This is why all Diakonia draws its power from faith in the Deacon Jesus Christ. Thus the social work of the Church is always dependent on the help of the Holy Spirit in order to be a witness to faith in love, that is: true Diakonia.

In this line the Bratislava declaration continues: "Diakonia, which is an essential aspect of Christianity, acts in the belief that poverty, unemployment and isolation are not inevitable." At the same time the Council of the Evangelical Church in Germany and the German Bishop's Conference have prepared the statement "For a Future Founded on Solidarity and Justice." The statement was published in 1997, it was prepared following a broad-based consultation process in the churches and their congregations, which went on since 1994. The publishers, the highest representatives of the Churches in Germany were full of sorrow. "Traditional social culture is undergoing great change due to industrialization and urbanization, and has in some points disintegrated. Material desires and selfishness are increasing and threatening solidarity and social cohesion. - Guided and encouraged by the Christian understanding of the human being, the biblical message and Christian social ethics, the churches want to make their contribution to the necessary reorientation of society. It is their concern to facilitate a common understanding of the foundations and perspectives of a public and social order that is humane, free, fair and based on solidarity. This should lead to a common effort being made to found the future on solidarity and justice. The churches do not see it as their task to give detailed political or economic recommendations. The chief task and competence of the churches is to advocate that which serves the cause of more equality and the common good…Yet solidarity and justice do not enjoy unmitigated respect nowadays. Individual selfishness is reflected in the tendency of social groups systematically to place their own interests before the common good. Some would like to take leave of the regulative concept of justice. This state of affairs is a great challenge to Churches and Christians, since solidarity and justice are at the heart of any biblical and Christian ethic."

I want to point out two aspects of the statement. It is, first, emphasized, that the churches are not a political party. "They do not aspire to political power in order to implement a specific programme. They consider themselves especially committed to advocacy for those who are easily forgotten in economic and political planning because they cannot speak out clearly themselves: the poor, the disadvantaged and powerless, coming generations, and dumb creatures. In this way they want to set the scene for political activity inspired by solidarity and justice."

And second: "In biblical and Christian tradition the churches have a treasure trove that can provide cultural enrichment in the future as in the past. They stand for a culture of mercy. The experience of divine mercy, from the liberation of Israel from Egypt, is the biblical foundation for the dual command to love God and our neighbor. Keeping the suffering of others in view is a condition for all culture. Mercy in the biblical sense is not a chance, fleeting feeling. The poor are meant to know mercy as a certainty. This mercy presses for justice."

Advocating in solidarity with the poor and standing for a culture of mercy this is the model of the Churches and Diakonia in Germany since then.

3. INCLUSION AND PARTICIPATION

In the German affluent society, the subject of poverty is still taboo, to a large intent. However, there is no ignoring the existence of poverty. Among others there are two special problems: The above-average risk of children falling into poverty is all the more worrying as being on the fringe of poverty can easily lead to different forms of lasting deprivation. Many people hide their poverty, i.e. they would be eligible for public assistance but they don't claim it for shame, lack of knowledge or fear of the authorities. This is called "covert poverty."

Christian love of the neighbor is primarily directed to the poor, the weak and the disadvantaged. The option for the poor becomes a benchmark for action. Life-enhancing dealings with the poor and the implementation of law and justice are signs of faithfulness to God's covenant. The reconciling encounter with the poor, in solidarity with them, becomes a place to encounter God. Therefore the statement of the German Churches 1997 underlined: The biblical option for the poor is aimed at overcoming exclusion and involving everyone in the life of society. Therefore volunteers are very important in protecting poor people against suspicion and discrimination.

In the following years a process of awareness rising in Diakonia lead to the concept of just participation. In the highly developed and affluent society like Germany, effectively tackling both extreme income poverty (income under the level of social assistance benefit) and poverty in the sense of inadequate participation in society and even defined as exclusion from society is an ethical imperative. The concept means the comprehensive involvement of everyone in education and training, economic activity, social security, and other expresses of solidarity. The Christian understanding of participation is anchored in a person's sharing in the divine reality, which is received as a gift from God. The Bible emphasizes inalienable human dignity and illustrates the conviction that each individual has been provided with the ability to participate actively, using symbolism such as that of the body of Christ (e.g. 1 Cor 12). It is each individual's responsibility before others and before God to take an active part in the society. The divine gift to us of participation in God must therefore translate into active work to shape our world. Therefore a just society must enable as many people as possible to recognize their individual talents, to develop them, and to use them productively for themselves and for others. With respect to today's economic system, this means that as many as possible should have gainful employment. By definition, the concept of just participation does not limit participation to only a few aspects of society. The concept will have to be carefully reviewed at regular intervals and reinterpreted in terms of practical action in today's world. So far "A Memorandum on Poverty in Germany: Just Participation. Empowerment for Personal Responsibility" published by the Council of the Evangelical Church in Germany 2006. The point of view was: In the face of new challenges there needs a greater focus on poverty in church-related and diaconal ministry.

The spirit of inclusion and participation is the new leitmotiv of the German churches since 2014, it is the next step of diaconal development with the purpose of decrease poverty. Poverty is a lack of economic, social, and cultural resources. Poor people in Germany remain poor much too often, and poverty is much too frequently passed on one generation to the next within families, especially within families with immigrant backgrounds. So it is a challenging task for social policy and the whole society, particularly for the Churches and Diakonia to make equal opportunity a reality. This involves allowing people with poorer social beginning to receive the support they need, from early childhood onward. Let me close with an encouraging example from the city of Tübingen, where my wife and I live. All children and minors of poor families get a so called KinderCard for free or reduced entry to open-air pool, theater and holiday offers, sports clubs, music lessons, language courses, private lessons.

> *"A kindly eye will earn a blessing, such a person*
> *shares out food with the poor."*

(PR 22,9)

Towards a Fair World

Evert Jan Hazeleger
Kerk in Actie, Netherlands

*"And when it was evening, his disciples came to him, saying, This is
a desert place, and the time is now past; send the multitude away,
that they may go into the villages, and buy themselves victuals. But
Jesus said unto them, They need not depart; give ye them to eat."*

St Matthew 14: 15-16

Kerk in Actie of the Protestant Church in the Netherlands and main activities.

The Protestant Church in the Netherlands with around 1.8 million members and 1600 local congregations is firmly rooted in the Dutch society. The Protestant Church is part of the world wide ecumenical 'body of Christ' on the local, national, European and global level. This includes partnerships with churches all over the world and membership of organizations like the Council of Churches in the Netherlands, the World Council of Churches, the ACT Alliance and all kinds of church and church-related networks.

The local congregations of the Protestant Church have their own missionary and diaconal work on the local level.

Kerk in Actie is the specialized ministry for missionary and diaconal work of the Protestant Church. Kerk in Actie is part of the Service Organization of the Protestant Church. We support the local congregations in their diaconal and missionary work and are working on behalf of the Protestant Church on a national and global level. On the global level Kerk in Actie works close together with ICCO a Dutch Christian Development organization. This organization was grounded 50 years ago to receive funding for development work from the Dutch government.

Kerk in Actie looks after the most vulnerable people, for people in need and for a more righteous world. Each human being has the right to respect and a dignified existence, irrespective of faith, political conviction, race, sex or nationality. Kerk in Actie is working to consolidate these rights, based on our Christian identity. In our work, Kerk in Actie seeks to follow the example of Jesus Christ, who calls to witness, to love our neighbors and seek for justice.

In the diaconal tradition the purpose and direction is in our key values: compassion, justice and stewardship.

Some characteristics of Kerk in Actie

Christian values

In stewardship the focus is on creating a sustainable society and protection and preservation of the entire creation; in compassion the focus is on being present where the ruptures are in society and be with the most vulnerable people and on the eradication of poverty; in justice the focus is on a more righteous world and the implementation of the three core values in the political, economic, financial and social structures of the society.

Diaconate is thus shaping the classic seven 'works of mercy' in a broad and comprehensive way, for the well-being and fullness of life of all the people and is handling a coherent agenda for the Global South as well as for the North.

PART OF THE ECUMENICAL NETWORK

Kerk in Actie is part of the international ecumenical networks of (protestant-Christian) churches, religious organizations and organizations allied to churches especially the WCC and the ACT Alliance. By preference we cooperate with organizations in these networks.

The strength of this network is that it is branched worldwide into small villages, in a multitude of organizations and reach all layers of the population. Within this network religious congregations can have direct relations with partner-congregations, often in small-scale projects. The relations in this partner network are in the first place of an ecumenical character and are deeper than merely financing projects. Kerk in Actie is not just another development agency which has as priority to channel the maximum of funds from North to South. Kerk in Actie focuses on linking people across the world and thereby showing that we are all created equal in the image of God.

PARTNERSHIP

Kerk in Actie is not only a funding organization or donor-organization but it is the diaconal work and missionary work of the Protestant Church. Kerk in Actie chooses to work from the perspective of partnership and to work together with churches and church related organizations with a substantial role for the local churches. Strategic aims and goals are defined together with partners. Partner conferences and the Regional Offices play a crucial role in this process.

To realize her goals Kerk in Actie actively seeks to work together with other organizations and with local groups and (grassroots-) movements with the same goals.

We want to be a reliable partner and want to remain present in politically and religiously sensitive areas and complex situations where there are fractures in society and changes cannot be realized at short notice. The network of our local (religious)partners enables us to be present there.

PARTNERSHIP WITH RECIPROCITY

There is more awareness of equality, the necessity for a critical dialogue and of the necessity to work and think in a shared responsibility of the various partners and with various actors striving for the same goals. Therefore partnership with reciprocity is essential in our work. We try to realize this in our programs. Through the support of local congregations in the Netherlands we promote direct involvement. Like exchange programs and a Youth travel program. This is important for living and understanding the diaconal and missionary calling as a Church. It strengthens the bond between the congregations of the protestant Church with the work of our partners and it creates the willingness to support this work in several ways.

COMMUNICATION

Kerk in Actie works by order of the Protestant Church and her congregations. It is therefore important that the local congregations recognize themselves in the work. Therefore a basic condition is good communication. We also want to reach and interest people outside of the Church. Therefore we also aim for those who want to shape their Christian inspiration in the 'service to the world', but have no formal connection with the church. The challenge is to show the value and the quality of our work to the Dutch society. In various campaigns (e.g. The lent Campaign) we focus on both the Church members and the broader Dutch public. We try to involve them in our work and ask for contributions for our work. In a combination of raising awareness and raising funds. The majority of the local congregations are actively involved in these campaigns.

COOPERATION

Kerk in Actie cooperates with ICCO and other organizations with a protestant background and vision. The execution of the foreign work takes place in the combined Regional offices and the International department of ICCO and Kerk in Actie.

Kerk in Actie and ICCO are complementary, reinforcing each other and recognizing each other's profile. In program development and –execution there is one combined approach. For world diaconal work this means amongst others a focus on poverty reduction and exclusion, with attention for the connection between social-cultural, economic, religious and political elements.

In fundraising ICCO contributes also the public funds and relations with other stakeholders, access to business and other back donors. Kerk in Actie aims basically on the private fundraising and on financing by the local congregations of the Protestant Church. Our yearly budget is 24 million euro. 40% comes from local Churches, 40% from individual donors and 20 % from private capital foundations. With this budget we are able to work in 40 counties including the Netherlands.

As the income of Kerk in Actie is under pressure for the last few years (between 2010 and 2014 a decrease of 5% yearly), we've worked on plans to try to increase the income from the congregations of the Protestant Church as well as from private donors. Because of this we've managed to get a slight increase of income from private donors. Beside this, a plan has been developed to work together with the congregations to focus more on fundraising for the diaconal work.

FUNDRAISING POLICY: A CLEAR CORPORATE STORY IS DEVELOPED.

Believing is sharing: Together we make up Kerk in Actie. We believe we're here to share with each other: that's how we embody the church in action and how we make it visible.

In our work we're inspired and touched by the story of Jesus and the five loaves and two fish. He blessed the food there was and shared it among the crowd – and there was enough for everyone.

Our calling: to share what we have received

We are the Protestant church in action.

- Around two million members and over 1600 local congregations are active on behalf of their fellow men and women, near and far.
- No one is excluded. All are welcome.
- We are touched and inspired by Jesus Christ and the Bible's call to take care of widows and orphans, prisoners and refugees. Kerk in Actie is committed to the most vulnerable people, to people in need and a more righteous world.

We believe that everyone is created in God's image, so we are all equal. Together we make up the body of Christ. This body knows no misfits: it has eyes and ears, hands and feet. Everyone is a part of this body in their own unique way: different, but always equal.

The church is in action everywhere: from the heart of Rotterdam – helping refugees to remote villages in Uganda- helping internally displaced people. Wherever people believe despite oppression, welcome refugees with open arms, stand up for children in need, care about minorities and embrace those who are excluded.

This clear corporate story helps us to be more visible for the church members and our donors. All workers of Kerk in Actie share this story and are trained to tell this story to our stakeholders, partners and donors.

OWNERSHIP AND THE STRENGTHENING OF THE CONNECTION WITH THE LOCAL CONGREGATIONS

Kerk in Actie is unable to do its work without a strong basis in the Dutch society. It was emphasized that Kerk in Actie works on behalf of and from the local parishes of the PCN. This was elaborated by directed cooperation in the field of local fundraising. Also the connection with the increasing number of donors of Kerk in Actie was intensified. We held a number of panel discussions with groups of donors. The conclusions of this study was used to strengthen the bond with our most important donors and local congregations.

The 40days - Lenten campaign with the theme "For a change" has been successful. This campaign was carried out together with more than 1100 congregations of the Protestant Church. Every year more and more congregations are getting involved in this campaign. In this campaign we make fundraising materials, background information about our work en we present each week one of our partners. Every year a new theme is chosen.

The 120th National Diaconal Day had as its theme "A heart for the Diaconate". It was about the bond between the input of diaconal work and worldwide challenges. More than a 1000 deacons attended the day. This day is held almost every year since 1891. This day is important for inspiration and sharing experiences.

ORGANIZATION: THE WORK IN 3 DEPARTMENTS

- Home department for the support of the diaconal work done by the 1600 congregations of the PCN. (3 mln)
- Mission department for our mission work and the support of mission work of our worldwide partner Churches and other partners. (10 mln)
- The worldwide diaconal program is part of the ICCO cooperation and is provided by the regional offices in Asia, Africa and Latin America. (11mln (including Humanitarian assistance)

WORKING AREAS OF KERK IN ACTIE

- Belief against oppression – supporting minority Churches – building Bridges between faith communities
- Belief in the power of local faith communities (food and economic empowerment, supporting the local diaconal work)
- Emergency relief, before, during and after disasters (DM)
- Migration, legal assistance to refugees, shave passage and shelter, combating human trafficking
- Children at risk – combating Child labor, strengthening Child rights

WORK OF THE HOME DEPARTMENT

You are here to see and learn from our diaconal work in the Netherlands. I will focus a little bit more on the work we do in the Netherlands. These are the diaconal themes we are working on in the Netherlands.

- Poverty reduction- advocacy, local support, helping people with debts.
- Refugees – humanitarian assistants, advising local congregations, showing best practices
- Sustainability – promoting sustainable lifestyle and praxis by Churches (Green Churches)
- Social Service – advocacy to local governments, Churches as a caring and providing community
- Support for the local diaconal work – good examples, training programs, pilot projects, newsletters, magazine for deacons, training on the job, tailored advice, conferences, e-learning programs.

In the Netherlands we've tried to seek more contact with the local diaconal work and we've tried to give more support to it. Focal points of the work were combatting poverty on a local level, supporting the deacons, attention for sustainability as a diaconal theme and to stand up for a humane asylum policy.

Successful local executed projects are:

- The network of parishes engaged with the "Schuldhulpmaatjes" (helping people who are in great debt). This network involves now more than 100 congregations and 1500 volunteers in our anti-poverty work.
- In the autumn of 2012 the first meeting took place within the framework of the so-called ''green churches''. One hundred and fifty people representing a large number of parishes attended. More than 100 local Churches and 900 volunteers are active in this network now.
- There was a frequent call for attention for the position of the asylum seekers and support was given to lobby activities and to individuals in urgent need of help. A network of local volunteers was grounded. We support them with a training on the job program and adequate information.

Good to know that most of the work is done by voluntary deacons in the local congregations. In the PCN there are about 10.000 Deacons and more than 100.000 other volunteers working for local diaconal work.

OUR APPROACH: WE CONNECT WE SHARE WE SUPPORT WE IDENTIFY

We connect: We serve the church in action worldwide by bringing together congregations, organizations and people who want to share what they have received. We establish contacts, for example by organizing a conference in Indonesia or a National Deacons' Day in the Netherlands.

We share: We serve the church by sharing what we have received: money, knowledge, experience and time. We do this at home and abroad. We encourage others to share too, for example by collecting money or by doing voluntary work.

We support: We serve the church by providing advice, inspiration and materials to people and congregations all over the world. Church social services, committees for global ministries and partner organizations can count on our commitment, staff and financial support.

We identify: We serve the church by identifying abuse and injustice worldwide. We expose these issues and act on them, thus acting as a voice for those who are not heard in the public and political arena.

Our areas of work: belief against oppression, belief in the power of local faith communities, emergency relief, migration and human trafficking, children in need and minority rights.

WE ARE NOT ALONE: THE IMPORTANT ROLE OF THE WORLD COUNCIL OF CHURCHES AND THE ACT ALLIANCE.

ACT is a worldwide Alliance with about 140 member organizations in more than 90 countries. Some members are national churches with special divisions which focus on humanitarian aid and development (like Kerk in Actie).

Together with ICCO, Kerk in Actie feels that the ACT Alliance should be the network of churches and church organizations in the field of the diakonia, development, humanitarian aid and advocacy. Within the ACT Alliance Kerk in Actie participated in joint emergency aid. Recently in Syria, Nepal and in other countries where immediate help was needed. Kerk in Actie and ICCO take part in a large number of national ACT forums in the 40 countries where ICCO and Kerk in Actie are active. In this way fragmentation can be prevented and by joining forces we can increase our strength.

'Think global and act local' is an expanding slogan. The entire inhabited world has become more and more one 'body'. What people do on a micro level matters and has an impact on a national and global level. And the other way around, the worldwide crisis in migration, economy, climate, food and access to raw materials demonstrates how hugely disastrous the impact of macro systems can be in the daily life of ordinary people.

Working within a worldwide Alliance makes the connections from local to local in a more complex world possible. In a world that becomes smaller and smaller, working together is more needed. The members of the church support Kerk in Actie but they are also critical towards the work. I think working together in the ACT Alliance makes better communication with the Dutch congregations and donors possible. Also in sharing the impact of our work. We can learn from each other. Also we are able to work more together towards a joint agenda for tomorrow regarding the highly needed lifestyle change of Countries and people. (for instance on climate change).

Development cooperation and Emergency aid is and will remain necessary, both in case of catastrophes and for the more vulnerable people who cannot help themselves right now. Although there is no doubt over this, it seems that the political motivation in Europe regarding partnership for development depends more and more on the question, whether it is profitable for ourselves and for our companies. Keeping what we have appears to be more important than fair sharing with each other!

Kerk in Actie, as a member of the ACT Alliance, is making a different choice and focuses on responsibility of partners, governments and the civil society to work in their individual context towards a more sustainable and righteous society.

A challenge for us the coming years is to hold on to the connection of compassion and justice, and to make sure that our work benefits the poorest and the most vulnerable. That's also the purpose of the Sustainable Development Goals on poverty. When we can hold on to that and find new ways to work together as an alliance than the ACT Alliance is successful and more visible (as Action by Churches and Christians Together).

TO CONCLUDE: WHAT'S MY DREAM FOR KERK IN ACTIE AS PART OF THE WORLD WIDE ACT ALLIANCE NETWORK.

That is a very big question! Almost too big in a world with the large international crises we are facing now. In a world unable to solve problems like the civil war in Syria, ongoing tensions between nations, the growing tensions between religions, the unjust of human trafficking and exploitation of migrants. In a world that cannot create sustainable systems of fair share, fair care, fair climate, fair trade and fair migration.

My dream is to make together steps in the direction of 5 times fair. Fair is my expression of systems that are in the core itself built on compassion, justice and stewardship. Become more FAIR is the diaconal agenda for the coming years.

Local action in a global society for fair share, fair care, fair trade, fair climate and fair migration is needed. The ACT Alliance makes it possible to work in this direction both in the north – Europe/ The Netherlands - and the global south.

The story of Christ feeds the five thousand is a great inspiration of myself and my organization. The end of this story shows the power of Christ and his lesson for us about sharing.

"And he commanded the multitude to sit down on the grass, and took the five loaves and the two fishes, and looking up to heaven,

he blessed, and brake, and gave the loaves to his disciples, and the disciples to the multitude. And they did all eat, and were filled, and they took up of the fragments that remained twelve baskets full."

ST MATTHEW 14: 19-20

That's the fullness of life with Christ.

DIACONAL WORK IN SWEDEN: SOME REFLECTIONS

Ninni Smedberg
Vårsta Diaconal Centre, Sweden

I WILL BRING GREETINGS from the Christian Council of Sweden, with 26 member churches that are divided into four church families. The Council links together the ministries and activities of the member churches by arranging forums for exchange of ideas, creating networks, giving communication service, providing support for developing ecumenism and coordinating joint activities.

CHALLENGES IN THE SWEDISH SOCIETY OF TODAY

The Swedish society has developed enormously the past few years, not only for the better. Also in our country, we face a development where an increasing number of people fail to get support from the social welfare, the gap between wealthy and poor is growing wider. Children are brought up in a situation of poverty (according to Swedish definition). Immigration and the increasing number of refugees are highly demanding, especially to small rural local authorities with limited economy.

Unfortunately, this has also lead to a significant increase of xenophobia and hostile attitudes towards vulnerable groups. Racist opinions and even a political party with a (hidden) racist agenda is part of the current political situation in Sweden.

The government, the state, has no longer a monopoly when it comes to welfare-service, (regulations of the European Union) entailing a growing market of private schools, hospitals and homes for care of old people. These private enterprises should mostly be purchased to the lowest price, meaning that the assignment or care itself is impoverished since private companies are making profit from what is actually run by means of common taxes.

During the period of construction of the welfare system, from the 1950s onwards, society was expected to provide most of the work of health-care, education and care, as a matter of public concern. Today Sweden like most of the rest of Europe, sees an ever-creasing number of actors within the areas of care and education. It is becoming increasingly frequent to find parishes or ecclesiastical institutions providing care either on the basis of grants for special project, or by delegation from the public sector.

Diaconal projects are example of efforts undertaken by ideologically based non-profit making organizations. These efforts and institutions belong within a sector that is neither public nor private, but which is sometimes called "the voluntary sector". In the EU-context, the terms the third sector, the social economy or the civil society are used.

The sector is frequently asked for and is expected to grow. By implication, this means that new choices and initiatives face parishes and diaconal institutions. It may be a request to act as a gathering force behind or together with various local actors. It may also be a request for the parish to sponsor various projects, such as institutions for care, rehabilitation, or cafés and maybe particularly in sparsely populated rural areas a post-office or a computer center.

The social debate about care and education in the future, often includes an invitation to the voluntary sector, precisely because it is not driven by any profit-making interest. And as an extra value there is mostly a group of people of good will connected to this work, sometimes as voluntary people.

TODAY THE CHURCH OF SWEDEN, AS WELL AS ALL OTHER CHURCHES IN SWEDEN, IS A CLEAR PART OF THE VOLUNTARY SECTOR.

Since the year 2000, when the strong link between the state and Church of Sweden was weakened, if not dissolved completely, the Church of Sweden is now part of the voluntary sector, "the third sector" and thus faces a new situation. The same situation as the rest of the other Churches in Sweden in an ecumenical perspective.

When it comes to the Institutes of Diakonia (City missions included) they are already involved and an active part of the Swedish welfare system of today. Sometimes with a clear assignment from the municipality or other authority (connected with money). Sometimes as an organization in the role of a lobbyist working with groups or individuals (often so called exposed/marginalized people) and not being paid for (using money from gifts and solidarity sponsoring). Trying in this work to be a voice together with exposed groups and individuals. Somehow the Institutes of Diakonia still fells that they are conducting a lot of diaconal service and social work not really acknowledge by the Church.

WHY DIAKONIA?

Firstly, the Theology of Creation. It is chosen because every work based upon a diaconal understanding is also based upon a holistic perspective, of the creation and of ever human mankind. It is of same importance locally as globally. All diaconal action needs critical reflection for the sake of the dignity of those involved, the needy, the suffering and the excluded.

Secondly, we can see that Jesus sets an example in how to relate to each other. Diaconal work wherever it is served should always be built upon a relationship, an act of liberation and reconciliation, of healing and lifting up the suffering, including the downtrodden and marginalized.

Thirdly, the ecclesiological perspective and the connection between diaconal institutions and the Church. Every diaconal institution reflect around how the relationship is formed and expressed towards a church body.

The body of Christ becomes visible in the Church in three different perspectives; when it witnesses to the mystery of God's love, when it gives thanksgiving to God in worship for the love made in manifest in Christ, and when it extends the love is has experienced to those beyond that network. These three perspectives are in fact different aspects of the church's mission.

DIACONAL WORK AND ACTIVITIES

There is a new openness, worldwide, for the role of religion in social and political matters. I can see a growing expectation from the society of an involvement from Churches and from diaconal institutions.

The Dictionary of the Ecumenical Movement defines Diakonia as "responsible service of the gospel by deeds and by words performed by Christians in response to the needs of people".

Firstly, Diakonia is action and cannot be limited to statements and good intentions. Diakonia contains deeds and words, formed as "responsible service" which means action for which one is accountable.

Diaconal work has also a focus, namely the needs of people. In the long tradition of the churches, Diakonia has therefore been linked to the situation of sick, poor and marginalized people, and has been carried out to accompany, help and defend people who are vulnerable.

Every diaconal action must therefore live in a balance between an understanding from a theological perspective (the connection to the Church) and from a perspective and understanding from the world around. That means listen to the tradition (to the roots) and being well connected to the context and the people.

It is important for me to say this with the connection between the word (preaching) and the action because the Churches in Sweden have been in the corner of preaching the gospel and have the diaconal action in a distance outside the church building… But lets go into the work now…

Traditionally, diaconal work has often been directed towards elderly, whether or not they have been previously known or active in the parish. Gradually, as an increasing number of parishes engage in analyses of the needs and in co-operation with other local agencies, the discussions about priorities become ever more prominent and new target-groups are identified.

New target-groups since some years are drug addicts, homeless people, poor families with children, single parents (specially mothers), young mothers, Romani people, baggers and the biggest challenge right now is all the refuges and "newcomers" to Sweden (escaping from war and poverty).

Every deacon, every congregation with a good diaconal work needs voluntary people actively taking part in diaconal actions. Some congregations have serval deacons or people employed responsible for the diaconal work, some congregations have one employed person and some congregation (specially where I come from North Sweden with small congregations in a geographically large area) have none. That means that the congregation itself have to organize its diaconal work depending on voluntary people.

So inside every congregation (no matter of domination) needs a leadership that is able to see the importance of holding the mission of the Church together as one (preaching and diaconal action). And inspire people inside the congregation to do a voluntary service inside the church, inspired by the gospel. My experiences is that most people want to do good and to cohere (to be part of a context, a need of belonging). Perhaps there is a need of a special diaconal leadership to inspire people to give of their skills, time and resources to other people. Voluntary people also have their needs, to feel that they can make a difference to someone, to feel that someone needs them, sees them and so on. It is to empower people. To conduct this groups of voluntary people inside congregations needs a leadership and a clear connection between a congregation inner life and the outreach work.

In our diaconal work/service, three different levels or foci, could be discerned:

1) To help. Reactive diaconal work.

Acute action of emergency. To support, e.g. with food, housing, money or clothing.

This work is growing and specially in our major cities. Our diaconal intuitions is very active, with employed people, with voluntary people, with money from the state and from solidarity money from people as gifts.

2) To give voice. Prophetic diaconal work.

The task of advocacy and change. Rights-based work, e.g. to accompany a person to the welfare-office to defend her/his legal rights. To speak out in protest, when structures, instead of meeting their intention, tend to become inhuman.

This work is also growing because of the growing gaps in the society and the fact that "ordinary people" also is being marginalized.

3) To restore. Proactive diaconal work. To be engaged in restoring the brokenness of creation. To liberate and care for the whole creation, humans as well as animals and environment, demands a way of long-plan thinking.

Diaconal work can be directed towards and carried out on the three levels:

Individuals – people must always find a refuge in the Churches, be seen and respected there and be offered well-considered help as the need arises.

Groups – by bringing people together, community may be created and the exchange of experience encouraged. People may then consider their own situation in a wider perspective and creativity, which can lead to the finding of solutions to problems being nourished.

Society – there are many ways to contribute to good social developments. The fundamental task is to participate in and to support the democratic assemblies and processes that already exist. Could it be that extra-parliamentary methods, lobbying or even civil disobedience might be necessary in order to challenge those in power who neglect their responsibilities? Many parishes have for example engaged in unusual practices in order to support refugees. The picture of diaconal work undertaken by parishes across the country may roughly be sketched like this: Care, Pastoral care, Treatment or Support.

Representatives for parishes and institutions diaconal work have a mission to put the visible, local needs, the expressions for human suffering, in a larger perspective. Then it is not sufficient to open a soup-kitchen or a shelter, just as it's not sufficient to help simply on an individual level (although, not questioning the value of this work). At the end of the day it is about help which empowers a human being and liberates strength rather than paralyzing feelings of subordination. It takes analysis of society and an internal discussion amongst the staff, within the parish or institution regarding how to prioritize. For example, concerning resource allocation within the budget, areas of responsibilities, who has the power to interpret the agenda, who's perspective is leading us in our diaconal work?

The deacon or someone appointed from a congregation, as the leader and source of inspiration of the diaconal responsibility of the congregation, must have a vocation and a mandate to be a critical voice, not only in society, but also towards a too self-occupied church. There has been a development, from "traditional" diaconal work, such as, home-visits, counselling, office hours, to an increasing focus on the rights-based perspective of the work. To represent those who are in an exposed and vulnerable position in life, means that you argue in favor of those without power, and you defend their human rights.

A political, prophetic Diakonia is about pointing out injustices wherever they are exercised. This shows the importance of theological reflection closely linked to the perspective of praxis.

It is an obvious challenge to the church to attack and fight against, unrighteous situations of life and the reasons and origin of this injustice, on a local, as well as on a global level. Prophetic Diakonia exercises faithfulness to the promise of the equal value of every human being and his/her dignity and sanctity. The prophetic vocation entails to reveal injustices and to fight for and defend justice, including human rights.

Diakonia has a call to build bridges, as well on the local as on the global level. Diaconal work should be a step ahead and maintain a holistic perspective – that is, to bring together, praise and grace with rights and justice and care.

GLIMPSE FROM MY OWN CONTEXT:

Vårsta Diaconal Centre is an independent foundation affiliated to the Church of Sweden with the aim of promoting Christian social and diaconal work. Vårsta is located in Härnösand, Sweden (in the middle of Sweden, 450 km above from Stockholm). We have 25 employed staff and about 10 people doing work as consultant.

- Develops practical diaconal and social work often in co-operation with others.
- A centre of diaconal knowledge, pastoral counselling and family counselling.
- Responsible for a crisis- and catastrophe center with national and international work, for ex psychosocial work in international disasters and work with people suffering from PTSS.
- Work with people that has been without work for a long time, also young people and refugees as well as with people with psychological handicap, called our green rehabilitation while it is conducted in a large garden.
- Work with people who needs work practice and for that we also hold a small social company.
- Running two homes for elderly (53 apartments), with no care like in a hospital but offers light support and encourage fellowship.
- Co-operates with churches, organizations and commercial companies.
- Offers a diaconal environment and have guest rooms as well as a conference center.

We cooperate with all congregations in the diocese mainly with our family counselling work. We have five centers were congregations can submit people (couples and individuals) in need of counselling. The diocese puts in some money and so do every congregation as well as there is a small fee for people. Secondly we also support and educate employed people in the congregations concerning how to handle crisis and catastrophe (in large as well as in small). This education is also open for people from other dominations (people employed by hospital, police or emergency service).

When it comes to global activities we support and educate all congregations of the Church of Sweden, both national and abroad, in how to handle crisis and catastrophes and acts of terrorism. We are also connected to a network of diaconal institutions inside Europe and the main activity inside that network in lobbyism and political social information.

We get a small among money from collections from some congregations or voluntary gifts from small groups inside congregations. We also get a small among money from individuals. But the major part of the money that makes the foundation running is money that we earn from projects or procurement (authorities or other is buying our services).

For example, we sell supervision to a lot of authorities (inside municipality as well as staff inside prions), we sell education to staff working with refugees and "newcomers" suffering from PTSS. We sell placements to employment office in the municipality for people that have been away from labor market and the work is about to help people find their motivation (and power) again (empowerment!).

We do not have a lot of voluntary people connected to our work, except for the board conducting the foundation. They support our work with putting in their expertise and time.

When we are asked to do so we conduct further education directed to voluntary people inside diaconal service inside congregations.

Our challenges of today are two folded:

Firstly, inside the Churches. There is a Swedish saying, "to have a stone in your shoe," meaning to become aware of something that is disturbing and unpleasant. It is part of the diaconal call and as well as diaconal institutions role to be a harsh eye-opener, a challenge to comfort, my own comfort and the comfort of the congregation and the Churches.

To most of us it is probably easier to gather and sing a hymn, listen to a sermon and pray together, rather than thinking about what the hymn, sermon and prayer actually challenge us to do. One among the tasks of the diaconal admission is to make the congregation aware of this connection (ora et labora), and arouse the question, how can I contribute my share?

This becomes strikingly obvious when someone responsible for diaconal work stands up during service pointing out local challenges, sometimes just outside the entrance of the church, - a temporarily living of baggers in the street, housing for asylum in a terrible condition, lacking almost everything that makes it a home, children at risk becoming homeless, poverty among elderly, scarcely having means for a proper meal a day. How often isn't it that we become blind to what is obvious?

The challenge of every congregation as well as a diaconal institution is to inspire and lead the members of the Churches to become a vibrant community, caring for each other in prayers as in praxis. This service will always challenge our comfort and there is a risk that we choose to close our ears and eyes.

And secondly the role of our diaconal institution is to call upon the needs of people in the society by marking out fields of work that "nobody" really is taking care of. Marking out were people (individuals or groups) is not being rightly taken care of.

Today we are fighting to be able to open a home/house for people arriving to Sweden right now with PTSS (new arrives migrants with trauma and other war damages). Especially young women with or without children and homosexuals. These categories are people suffering most also arriving to Sweden and forced to live in sometimes bad conditions (together with mostly young men from all over the world). Our aim is to have a home were we also can offer treatment, psychological social support etc.

So for me as the director of Vårsta the challenge is always to listen to the call from God as well as what the context (the society and people of today) demands from us.

LOVE IN ACTION: A REFLECTION ON AMITY'S WORK

Zhao Jingwen
The Amity Foundation, China

THE AMITY FOUNDATION is an independent Chinese voluntary organiza-tion founded in 1985 on the initiative of Chinese Christians and support of interested groups to promote education, social services, health, community development, environment protection, disaster relief, and poverty reduction in the underdeveloped areas of China. Amity projects have benefited more than ten million people both at home and abroad. In 2014 the Amity Foundation was granted the special consultative status by the United Nations' Economic and Social Council (ECOSOC).

Abiding by principles of mutual respect and interfaith harmony, Amity builds friendship with people at home and abroad. Through the promotion of holistic development and public welfare, Amity serves society, benefits the people, and contributes to world peace.

Amity projects have focused on community governance through promot-ing rural community integrated development projects and urban community service. Our working areas include, but not limited to, primary education, environmental protection, and assistance to particular disadvantaged groups. With thousands of such projects, sustainable development in the project areas has been enhanced.

1. AMITY'S PRACTICE

RURAL COMMUNITY DEVELOPMENT

COMMUNITY DEVELOPMENT AND ENVIRONMENT PROTECTION

Amity has implemented over 30 Rural Integrated Development Projects in Hunan, Yunnan, Sichuan, Guizhou, Guangxi, Inner Mongolia, etc., helping establish more than 200 farmers' autonomous organizations, playing an active role in encouraging villagers participation in community construction. Project implementation items, including capacity building, education, health care, farming infrastructure, returning cultivated land to grassland and forests, animal husbandry, green and recyclable energy and cultural preservation have led to ongoing improvement in community economy, eco-environment, health care, education, cultural heritage, and community reconstruction and sustainable development, benefiting a target population of nearly 6 million.

PUBLIC HEALTHCARE AND HIV-AIDS PREVENTION

Based in rural communities, Amity projects have attempted to combine disease prevention and healthcare in integrated community service with an eye to building primary health care networks. To date, these public healthcare and HIV-AIDS prevention drives have run training workshops for 16,000 village doctors and 6,900 township hospital workers in 9 provinces in west China, helped establish hundreds of village clinics in poverty-stricken regions, and launched prevention and treatment campaigns for diseases like iodine deficiency disorder (IDD) and gynecological disease. From the mid-1990s, a series of anti-HIV-AIDS projects were implemented in communities in Yunnan, Henan, Hunan, Guizhou provinces, Guangxi Zhuang Autonomous Region, and Chongqing Municipality, distributing free anti-virus drugs, peer education among sex workers, micro-credit to People Living with HIV/AIDS, and advocating safe sex behavior to people at high risk and juvenile groups, in order to probe new ways of HIV/AIDS prevention and cure.

SCHOLARSHIP AND ORPHAN FOSTERING

The Amity Foundation has never ceased its attention to disadvantaged rural school-age children. Back to School has provided support for 120,000 middle and primary school children. Project Torch has supported 900 financially-challenged students throughout their college years. With our funding, at least 700 middle and primary schools have had their campuses not only rebuilt or renovated, but also received improved teaching facilities, activity rooms, solar shower rooms, physical exercise and music rooms. Amity's Orphan Fostering has financed schooling for 13,000 orphans and attempted to carry out psychological care for orphans.

SOCIAL WELFARE

Our social welfare endeavors have stressed medical and educational services for the disadvantaged in social communities, involving 4 major sectors in 12 provinces and regions, namely, collaborative projects with orphanages, special education, medical treatment and rehabilitation and hospice care. Amity has carried out training for eye doctors and eyecareworkers, supported over 100 mobile medical teams of cataract surgeons, with tens of thousands of patients served. Amity also supported rehabilitation therapy for 1400 polio victims, scholarships to disabled children, and integrated education for visually impaired children. The pilot bilingual education projects undertaken in several provinces have reached the international leading level.

URBAN COMMUNITY SERVICE

URBAN COMMUNITY SENIOR SERVICE

Amity Rengu Nursing Home, directly managed by the Foundation, was set up in 2012 under the Civil Affairs Bureau of Qixia District, Nanjing. With a construction area of 10,000 square meters and 240 beds, it has adhered to the mission of offering "individualized and whole-person care". Through the adoption of proficient models of management and service, Rengu is now housing a comprehensive service team made up of social work professionals, nurses, therapists, and caretakers. We have also served seniors service in more than 10 neighborhoods in the vicinity of Rengu, who count on our professional support and on the Virtual Nursing Home — another Amity project. Through incorporating home, community and institution-based care, we have been exploring and practicing a multi-channel senior service system. Recently we signed an agreement with Jiangsu People's Hospital to co-found, over the next three years, a pioneering elderly care center integrating medical-residential-caring services.

SERVICE FOR DISABLED JUVENILES

As the first professional non-profit institution in Nanjing, Amity Home of Blessings is dedicated to provide training in skills for daily life, community adaptation and various vocational settings. It received an award as a "Model Shelter & Care Facility" in Jiangsu Province in 2010 from the Jiangsu Disabled Persons' Federation. The Amity Bakery has been functioning as a professional, safe and fair vocational training base. The above-mentioned efforts, coordinated and backed up by social resource mobilization, will avail trainees a platform for earning their own lives with dignity. The Bakery, as a recipient of the "Pilot Non-Government Social Service Institution" award from the China Association of Social Work, has now been transformed into a social enterprise whose advocacy and innovation has received extensive recognition at home and abroad.

REHABILITATION SERVICE FOR CHILDREN WITH AUTISM

In 2008, to address the developmental and educational challenges confronting children and their families, we set up the Amity Children Development Center to provide professional assessment, rehabilitation, early intervention and support as well as training and group activities for autistic children and students in primary and junior middle schools and their caregivers. In 2014, the center was appointed by the provincial Disabled Persons' Federation as the sole institution qualified to host rehabilitation training for children ages 7 to

14 in Gulou District, Nanjing. Additionally, six international symposiums on autism have been important in spurring exchanges and sharing of medical, therapeutic and caregiving expertise and experience.

DISASTER MANAGEMENT

In response to the fire in the Greater Xing'an Mountains in 1987, Amity launched its first-ever disaster relief project — the Greater Xing'an Mountains Construction Reward Fund. Since then, Amity has responded to an average of 2-3 natural disasters every year and has made relief efforts in over 50 major natural disasters, including the floods in East China in 1991, the Yangtze River flood in 1998, and the Wenchuan earthquake in 2008. Amity has left its disaster-relief footprints in more than 20 Chinese provinces, as well as in North Korea, Kenya, the Philippines and Nepal.

After the Wenchuan earthquake in 2008, Amity launched a community reconstruction project at Woyun Village in Mianzhu County. The project mobilized the participation of earthquake-affected villagers, aiming to explore a new path of post-disaster reconstruction through both material aid and spiritual support. In April 2015, Amity's prompt relief response to the earthquakes in Nepal was a landmark in Chinese non-profit organizations' involvement in international relief efforts.

INTERNATIONAL EXCHANGES AND COOPERATION

The education and international exchange programs aim to provide equal education opportunities for vulnerable groups and promote intercultural exchanges. Encouraging young people to participate in social services, the programs provide young adults at home and abroad with a platform covering overseas study, volunteering, internship, and interpersonal networking opportunities. With the goal of building the younger generation's competence in knowledge, volunteerism and innovation, young adults in these programs are imbued with an international view and caring humanism.

For 30 years, these programs attracted more than 2,000 long-term foreign teachers to teach English in colleges in China. The Summer English Program trained over 32,000 Chinese teachers from primary and secondary schools. Thousands of young adults from the United States, Denmark, Germany, Norway, Australian, Japan and other countries, as well as Hong Kong SAR volunteered with the Service Learning Program, which promoted exchanges between Chinese and foreign youth.

For 30 years, Amity has directly received thousands of overseas friends who came to China for cooperation, study and visits. Just during the last ten years, Amity has been visited by many worldwide Christian leaders, including the General Secretary of the World Council of Churches, two Archbishops of Canterbury, the General Secretary of the World Evangelical Alliance, the Global South Archbishops, and the Nigerian Bishops. In 2013, US ambassador Gary Locke and Mrs. Sharon Johnston, the wife of the Governor General of Canada, visited the Amity Bakery. In recent years, major foreign media, including ARD Fernsehen, BBC, CNN, the Los Angeles Times, the Chicago Tribune, and The Financial Times, conducted interviews and reported on the Amity Foundation. As a member of China NGO Network for International Exchanges, Amity actively participated in exchange and cooperation with Africa and was granted special consultative status with the Economic and Social Council of the United Nations in 2014. Amity's non-governmental diplomacy efforts have not only widened its international perspective but also promoted understanding and communication between China and other countries and made contributions to people-to-people friendship and world peace.

2. RELIGIOUS PHILANTHROPY

Bishop K. H. Ting and other church leaders made great efforts to adapt Christianity to Chinese conditions making the development of the Church fit with Chinese socialist society. They held that Christians should not only focus on personal salvation but also show their humanistic care to vulnerable groups. Thus the Amity Foundation was established in 1985 with this original intention becoming a demonstration and window of Chinese churches' social service, hoping Chinese Christians to get more involved in social affairs of China and contribute to the country's reform and opening-up process and letting society know more about Christianity and Christians.

A prominent difficulty for churches to participate in social service lies in the contradiction between churches' religious features and China's no proselytizing policy. In 1980s, China was just at the beginning of its social service work while Chinese churches had the responsibility of helping Chinese Christians in poverty. Establishing a social service agent like the Amity Foundation when there was no well-written law to stipulate churches how to conduct social service work provided a good opportunity for common people to better know and accept Amity's service under China's actual conditions. It started a new way for Christianity to get localized in China and was an attempt for it to provide social service with Chinese characteristics.

As a Christian initiated NGO, one of Amity's goals is to make Christian involvement and participation in meeting the needs of society more widely known to the Chinese people. Amity strives to hasten the involvement of Chinese religious circles, especially Christians, in social construction and to upgrade their social service capacity to meet the increasing needs of society.

CHURCH AND SOCIAL SERVICE

Since 2002, Amity has supported over 210 church-run social service projects with a total investment of 100 million yuan, benefiting 300,000 people, mainly in central and western China. By the end of 2015, more than 80 non-government social service organizations mostly from Jiangsu and ten other provinces, including Shandong and Anhui, have joined the social service network, mainly consisting of church social service organizations.

JIANGSU CHRISTIAN FUND FOR SOCIAL SERVICE

With support from the United Front Work Department of CPC Jiangsu Committee and Jiangsu Religious Affairs Bureau, Amity and Jiangsu TSPM/CC jointly founded Jiangsu Christian Fund for Social Service. The fund focuses on rural health, environmental protection, children development, service for disability, church volunteer team building and social service capacity building, and so on. The fund implements capacity building projects as project management, service for the elderly and the handicapped. The Fund has raised over 20 million yuan, supported 138 social service projects of 22 categories and benefitted over 100,000 people. Among others, Church Environmental Protection Action has carried out 24 environmental protection events in 9 places in Jiangsu attracting over 46,000 Christian participants.

INTERFAITH COOPERATION

Entrusted by the United Front Work Department of CPC Jiangsu Committee and Jiangsu Religious Affairs Bureau, Amity held the first Jiangsu Religious Philanthropy Training Workshop in July 2015. It was attended by more than 60 leaders from the five major religions in Jiangsu. The five-day workshop focused on both theory and practice achieving good results and scored a first in China by providing a platform for inter-religious dialogue and philanthropic cooperation, winning wide acclaim from religious circles in China and overseas. Amity's role as a bridge and platform for religions to be involved in social service development has become increasingly important.

3. COOPERATION AND RESOURCE DEVELOPMENT

The allocation of resources has been the strong backing for each of Amity's successful transformations. Amity's 20th anniversary, a decade ago, was the first time Amity had raised more than 100 million RMB in a year. We were encouraged. Yet, Amity's astute management personnel perceived a crisis. As China's comprehensive national strength continued to improve and developed countries overseas experienced an economic slowdown, it was dangerous to rely on overseas resources for 95% or more of Amity's funding. It is gratifying that Amity's domestic fund raising has continually exceeded from overseas for the past 4 years, and that Internet philanthropy, philanthropy for all, special funds, and others have become new resource gathering platforms.

Amity works closely with overseas partner to raise fund for the project. In the past 30 years, Amity received a lot of care and support from friends at home and abroad. In the recent years, Amity feels its responsibility to contribute to the outside world. Amity supported earthquake in Nepal, flood in Philippines, flames in the African. On the Amity website, there is a regular fund raising project for the medical support for Africa people. We raise fund domestically and support the people outside of China. Financially speaking, Amity has transformed resource structure to guarantee Amity's sustainable development. Last year Amity's domestic fund is 76% of total funding.

Philanthropy goes beyond borders, languages, and ethnic groups. Presently, as never before, people are aware that the planet they live on has long been an interdependent community, sharing the same fate. In the past three decades, Amity's development has always gained strong support from many friends and partners at home and abroad. The Amity of today would not exist without universal sharing. Therefore, Amity has the responsibility and obligation to enable ecumenical sharing of its practice and achievements through South-South cooperation and South-North cooperation. "I do not consider that I have made it my own. But one thing I do: forgetting that lies behind and straining forward to what lies ahead, I press on towards the goal for the prize of the upward call of God in Christ Jesus" (Philippians 3:13-14)

There is a long way ahead. Amity needs the continuous support of more friends and partners at home and abroad. If you walk alone, you walk fast; if you walk together, you walk further. Amity hope to walk with all of you hand in hand in light of Amity's mission and vision to achieve more abundant lives, more justice, and a better world!

Empowering Diakonia to Overcome Poverty

Carlos E. Ham
Theological Evangelical Seminary in Matanzas, Cuba

1. Introduction

As churches, committed to social justice, like those gathered here, the main theme of this International Seminar on Diakonia, namely *'No Poverty' of the UN Sustainable Development Goals*, is indeed very relevant, if we want to be consistent with our Christian faith, particularly to the diaconal ministry of our Lord Jesus Christ.

In the Latin America tradition of Theology of Liberation, rather than dealing with the notion of poverty, as 'the state of being extremely poor', the term better used is impoverishment, focusing on the process by which people are being deprived of resources, mainly as the result of unjust structures. Therefore, as churches we are called to be better aware of causes and consequences of poverty, beyond the charity mentality, in order to accompany the destitute in concrete actions of solidarity. Hence, diaconal action, by definition ought to be prophetic, namely to comfort the impoverished and at the same time to confront the root causes of injustice.

2. Diakonia in the Ecumenical Movement

The ecumenical movement in general and the WCC in particular, through its member churches, have had a very strong involvement in diaconal work throughout the 20th Century and up to the present days, both in reflection and in practice. In this area, I have been observing three phases or models of ecumenical diakonia that I have identified throughout this rich history, finding paradigm shifts. These phases will sometimes show conflicting signs or moments of tension and in other occasions, complementing trends among each other. The phases or models, which will be explained below, are the *charity*, the *reciprocity* and the *transformative* models.

a) ***The charity model***. This is the *inter-church aid* period, characterized quite prominently by the transfer of funds in a rather vertical, top-down way, to support diaconal projects and persons in need. To a great extent, people were seen as *objects* of the aid, coming from the most powerful churches and church-related organizations, primarily from the global North. Diakonia was defined in this period as the "responsible service of the gospel by deeds and by words performed by Christians in response to the needs of people".[2] This charity model runs from the early 20th Century up until the beginning of the 1980s and its effect is help.

b) ***The reciprocity model***. This phase is represented by the *Ecumenical Sharing of Resources* [3]process,[4] which was developed in the 1980s, primarily by the 1986 Global Consultation on Inter-Church Aid, Refugee and World Service, *Diakonia 2000. Called to be Neighbors*, held in Larnaca (Cyprus) and the 1987 El Escorial (Spain) Consultation on *Koinonia*. During this period, I start to observe a paradigm shift, mostly as a result of the presence and influence of voices and ministries from the churches in the global South and East. Here I begin to see emerging the notions and practices of empowerment in relation to diakonia.

---

2 Teresa Joan White, "Diakonia," in *Dictionary of the Ecumenical Movement*, ed. by Nicholas Lossky et al, 2nd. edn (Geneva: WCC Publications, 2002), accessed on 15 September 2013, <www.oikoumene.org>, p. 305.

3 Dong-sung Kim, 'Partnership and Resource Sharing', *Ecumenical Missiology. Changing Landscapes and New Conceptions of Mission*, 35 (2016), pp. 259–70.

4 Carlos Ham, 'Historical Review of the Sharing of Resources Within the Ecumenical Movement. Presented at the International Consultation on the Relationship Between Churches and Specialized Ministries / 4–10 September 2014, Nkopoloa Lodge, Malawi.' (Not published).

In this model, which runs up to the first decade of the 21st Century, in a more intentional and collective way there is an assessment of the needs, the challenges and the problems, also on a more horizontal level. E.g. the participants at the Larnaca consultation underscored in their final Declaration "…Our diakonia now and for the future must be based on mutual trust and genuine sharing. We recognize that people and churches on all continents have needs and that our diakonia must reach out to all those who suffer".[5] Also at the El Escorial consultation there was a deliberate attempt to overcome the false dichotomy between mission and service, within the *Life and Work* framework. Its report acknowledges, "All activities of the Christian community in evangelism, diakonia, the struggle for human dignity, healing, peace and justice belong together in the one mission of God".[6] Nevertheless, I observe in this period that the *we-they* mentality is still quite prominent, while at the same time, there is a stronger emphasis on resources other than financial, e.g. human, that are expected to be shared. The effect of this trend is moving towards change.

c) ***The transformative model.*** The process leading to the 2012 Conference on *Theological Perspectives on Diakonia in the Twenty-First Century*, held in Colombo, Sri Lanka, marks this period that I call *transformative*. There is a stronger influx in relation to the notion of diaconal practice from the different WCC related mission networks and not least from the persons quite often excluded by society and even by the churches. This further worked towards achieving inclusivity and integration of the different diaconal efforts, a stronger relationship *to-each-other*; done by those from the periphery, by those on the margins (disabled, women, indigenous people, afro-descendants, impoverished), empowered to change society in a *bottom-up* approach, in an inductive manner. The effect of this model is transformation.

---

5   Klaus Poser, *Diakonia 2000 – Called to Be Neighbors. Official Report of the WCC World Consultation on Inter-Church Aid, Refugee and World Service, Larnaca, Cyprus, November 1986* (Geneva: World Council of Churches, 1987), p. 125.

6   Hubert van Beek, *Sharing Life in a World Community. Official Report of the WCC World Consultation on Koinonia, El Escorial, Spain, 1987* (Geneva: WCC Publications, 1989), p. 45.

3. DIAKONIA AND EMPOWERMENT

The same year of the Colombo Conference, the WCC held a *Seminar on Empowerment for Diakonia in Central America and the Spanish-Speaking Caribbean*, at our Theological Evangelical Seminary in Matanzas, Cuba. In the final statement the participants noted:

> Diakonia must be based on ethical, social, political, environmental, legal and inter-cultural values, be faithful to the churches' overall mission, and be inclusive in its activities, bringing together young people, children and women. Also diaconal service must promote processes enabling individuals to be capable of changing their situation and of promoting the principles of an economy that is inclusive, in the form of cooperatives and associations.[7]

Reading this quote, I can highlight the following observations in relation to our topic, namely, (1) first and foremost, this diaconal endeavor is performed by the churches as part of God's mission; (2) it is interdisciplinary, involving various sciences and partners; (3) that it is inclusive, embracing all sectors of the community, not only of the congregations; and finally (4) it is empowering, enabling participation and agency for change, since, as the Statement goes on to say: "Diakonia is not conducted from a stance of absolute power, but out of power devoted to the common good. 'Serving', as an act of convenience or of absolute power, is contrasted with the meaning of service in the biblical sense".[8]

Therefore, there is a close relationship between diakonia and empowerment, acknowledging the latter as a dynamic process that enables and inspires, that enhances people's skills and self-confidence; it is a movement by which persons liberate, take back and develop the power within, in order to *unlock*

---

7 WCC, *Final Statement of Seminar on Empowerment for Diakonia in Central America and the Spanish-Speaking Caribbean, Matanzas, Cuba - 15-20 July 2012* (Matanzas, Cuba, 2012), p. 2.

8 WCC, *Final Statement of Seminar on Empowerment for Diakonia in Central America and the Spanish-Speaking Caribbean, Matanzas, Cuba - 15-20 July 2012*, p. 3.

their immense potential and to boost their skills, self-confidence and self-assertion. This process aims at promoting collective resistance, challenge and mobilization against dominating power relationships and systemic forces that impoverish and exclude the vulnerable people, towards positive changes in the situations where they are living, by creating justice, inclusiveness and participation towards transformation and righteousness.

In the ecumenical movement several quotes can be found that point to the crucial relationship between empowerment and diakonia, by which there is a cross-fertilization among the two, i.e. a call can be found for the churches to work towards achieving empowerment to lift human dignity, self-sustainability and transformation by the own people. An outstanding example can be this one: "Empowerment is at the heart of diaconal and justice-seeking activities and can be seen as an overarching characteristic or goal of much of the work of the churches and church-related organizations. Empowerment activities in a Christian framework address the dignity of humanity and reveal to each person and group their inherent gifts and abilities so that they may actively work towards transformation".[9]

One of my basic assumptions is that, from the perspective of the Judeo-Christian tradition, empowerment is encouraged to take place in mutuality, in partnership, in a spirit of power-sharing, a process of reaching out to the other with the love of the triune God and is, therefore intrinsically attached to diakonia, which affirms the power-service in Christ's way. Nowadays many local churches are being empowered for diaconal work as a result of their ecclesial condition and urged by the needs of the people. Consequently, empowerment and diakonia are integral parts of being a missional church; people are emerging *self-empowered* for action becoming, beyond being objects of aid and charity, being subjects of their own destiny and of their respective communities.

So the issue here, as we address the challenge of impoverishment, is not to help the poor just to solve their needs, rather, to facilitate an empowerment process by which they can be part of the solution and not only part of the

---

9 WCC, *Diakonia: Creating Harmony, Seeking Justice and Practising Compassion* (Geneva, 2005), p. 7.

problem. One way of doing this is by implementing what I call the *Empowering Diakonia* model. This can be an essential tool not only to interrelate both the theory and practice, but also as a helpful diagnosis instrument for analysis, description and interpretation for practical implementation. Hence, the application of the model, as it interrelates both diakonia and empowerment, helps us to move from practice to theory and back to practice for transformation.

4. THE *EMPOWERING DIAKONIA* MODEL

The *Empowering Diakonia* model can be defined as the driving force that leads, in our case the churches, particularly local congregations, towards self-fulfillment of those in need, to develop as social actors. The churches are called to renounce any power *over* people, but rather through God's power to serve *with* the people, through acts of effective love, and serving human needs, for individual and social transformation for mutuality and justice. Of course, this empowerment process is not limited to the congregations, but also includes other religions and the wider communities.

The model is composed by five elements, called the *Five Dimensions of Empowering Diakonia*, which include the following: visional, normative, need-oriented, contextual and transformative; and are both interdisciplinary and interrelated. In the following section a summary of the meaning of each will be noted:[10]

A. Visional – referring to the ability of envisioning future reality so as to consider action with imagination and wisdom. The vision motivates, like the view of utopia that *causes us to advance*,[11] it is the engine, and the ideo-

---

10   Carlos Ham, *Empowering Diakonia: A Model for Service and Transformation in the Ecumenical Movement and Local Congregations*, PhD Thesis - Free University of Amsterdam (Amsterdam, Netherlands, 2015), pp. 15-17.

11   This quote is from Eduardo Galeano (1940-2015), a Uruguayan journalist, writer and novelist, who expressed: "Utopia lies at the horizon. When I draw nearer by two steps, it retreats two steps. If I proceed ten steps forward, it swiftly slips ten steps ahead. No matter how far I go, I can never reach it. What, then, is the purpose of utopia? It is to cause us to advance". Website accessed on 5 January 2014, http://www.goodreads.com/quotes/33846-utopia-lies-at-the-horizon-when-i-draw-nearer-by

logical foundation. According to the Judeo-Christian tradition this is crucial since "where there is no vision, the people perish" (Pr. 29:18). Furthermore, a diaconal vision is inspired and empowered by God the Father, the Son and the Holy Spirit. It relates to theological reflection, to spiritual-mystical experiences, and to liturgical practices, towards a critical analysis of reality and action, an imagination of what is feasible, seeking to achieve *another possible world*.[12] Hence, "In a theological perspective, empowerment has a God-given goal (*telos*) of energizing people in God's project and realizing God's good intention for creation and human society: of mutual love and care, and of promoting human dignity and justice".[13] Therefore, the vision is seeking empowerment and, at the same time, empowers, in this case, for diaconal action.

B. Normative – deriving from a standard or norm, particularly of behavior and therefore has ethical connotations. It is a commanding point of reference, of taking stances, which provides meaning for the actions of a particular group. It is expressed in human core values, principles, and standards of comportment, in the judgment of what is important in life. In the particular Judeo-Christian tradition, it is rooted in the authority of the biblical text, but at the same time it reflects professional effectiveness. As diaconal engagement is not an option, but part of the essence of being church, *condition sine qua non*, it is normative, essential for its mission, and therefore a faith-based empowered and empowering service.

C. Need-oriented – pointing both to material and spiritual necessities of the people requiring some course of action, focusing on the causes (asking not only what the needs are, but also why they are present in the first place) and consequences of such needs. They identify processes of empowerment and require the churches' social intervention, in order to comfort the people in need, and also to confront prophetically the powers that destroy the web of life. This dimension also considers the needs of the churches in order to address effectively and jointly the necessities of the communities, following the

---

12 Website accessed on 18 February 2015, http://www.forumsocialmundial.org.br/index.php?cd_language=2

13 Kjell Nordstokke, 'Empowerment in the Perspective of Ecumenical Diakonia', *Diaconia*, 3 (2) (2012), p. 194.

ministry of Jesus Christ, who was moved by the needs of the people. Hence, when his followers see the needs of others, their values are activated, from a perspective of solidarity and effective love.

D. Contextual – considering a theology and a praxis that are contextual, the churches' diaconal involvement is concerned and empowered in a particular setting, committed to the community, society in general –addressing economic and political issues- and the environment. The context provides the critical elements to assess more accurately the reality in order to exercise an interdisciplinary engagement, together with other actors and sciences. It helps to focus and fine-tune empowering action that regenerates the lives of the people.

E. Transformative – lifting a diaconal pro-action that aims at the ultimate goal of reaching *koinonia* through transformation, building inclusive communities of justice and peace that include all people. It is an open-ended creation process, where the church and other agents of change co-laborate with God, in order to incarnate the values of the Kingdom and provide fullness of life for all creation. Hence, from the theological point of view, it is seen as open-ended, since God is responsible for the ultimate outcome or result, providing newness of life. Therefore, it is an expression of the church's faith in God, and consequently it should be dealt with humility and confidence in God's plan. For this, it is important to pursue the transformation of the churches themselves, experiencing first powerlessness, *kenosis*, by picking up the cross and following in the footsteps of the *Suffering Servant*, as an empowering process to reach *koinonia*.

In other words, this flow of the *Five Dimensions*, help us to move from a practical informed vision, taking normative stances to address effectively and prophetically the needs of the people, in their various contexts, towards transformation and justice.

5. CUBA - A PRACTICAL EXPERIENCE

Cuba is a *sui generis Third World* country. Its Socialist system, even with its shortcomings, has tried to be a moral authority for more than half a century, since, unlike other similar political systems in Eastern and Central European countries, it carried out a victorious Revolution that triumphed in 1959, against the regime of Fulgencio Batista. At the same time, Cuba has suffered one of longest embargoes, imposed by the US Government, which has been condemned by the great majority of the world's nations and by various United Nations General Assemblies. After the collapse of the Berlin wall and since the early 1990s, when the country's *Secular Constitution* was adopted, the churches have been carrying out their mission no longer confined to the four walls of the sanctuaries, rather, extended throughout the Cuban society.

In this country there are signs of changes taking place where various churches[14] are playing an important role in the society to improve the quality of life of the people. The diaconal mission of these churches has gained a new momentum, primarily for the following reasons: (a) the growing improvement of the relations between the state and the churches, by which the latter have more freedom to carry-out their mission; (b) the needs of the population have increased as a result of the economic crisis; and (c) as a consequence of the decentralization of the economy by the state, which challenges the civil society in general.

We have made some research among various Cuban ecumenical churches and as a result, the *Five Dimensions of Empowering Diakonia* can be described in these terms, as an example of how they can be worked on:

1. **Vision**. There is a shared vision embedded in their identity as churches, which provides the necessary impulse and commitment for diaconal actions. In my view, this vision lifts empowerment in order to meet creatively the challenges of the Cuban churches, which in many cases are playing an important *pathfinding* role.

2. **Normative**. Acknowledging various biblical texts, the churches are morally obliged to serve, ecumenically when possible, the most vulnerable, following the example of Jesus, who helped unconditionally those in need.

---

14 Basically I am referring here to the mainline historical Protestant churches, that belong to the Council of Churches and send their students to our Theological Evangelical Seminary. Nevertheless, as it happens in other countries, we are facing a growing charismatic movement which, among other issues, are not interested in social engagement.

3. **Needs.** The Cuban churches are challenged by the needs of the population and are called to address them holistically, providing both material support as well as meaning and hope for the lives of the people. At the same time, the churches face needs themselves, mainly in the area of competence, in order to address these necessities in the society, in a sustainable manner.

4. **Context.** In the changing situation in Cuba, the *historical* churches (mainline Protestant and Roman Catholic) are playing a more active role in their setting, e.g. in the area of diakonia; the civil society in general is becoming a stronger actor in moments when poverty is increasing. In this context, discernment and courage are required by the churches to fulfill this mission.

5. **Transformative.** Moving towards the future, several transformative priorities for Cuba in the area of diakonia were identified, namely, strengthening the initiatives of capacity building for diakonia; enabling ecumenical networking of churches and interreligious cooperation with diaconal projects; and reinforcing dialogue among the churches, the state and with other social actors in the area of service. The Cuban churches as *pathfinders* are living a very important *kairos*, a crucial and critical time to bear witness to the living Christ, both in words and in deeds. They are becoming relevant actors in the Cuban society as agents for transformation, empowerment and reconciliation, further developing a sense and commitment to justice and dignity. Consequently, the churches are playing a very active role as pioneers, helping to discover a new course or way, re-orienting in order to promote better human and social relationships.

In other words, reflecting on the results of this research, it becomes clear that the concept of *diakonia as pathfinder* is central in Cuba's present *kairos* as expressed in the *Five Dimensions*. The Cuban churches are called to play this role in diakonia, as humble service, juxtaposed with servility towards the state and other powers. Consequently, they are empowered not only to serve the most vulnerable people, but also being proactive in prophetic engagement, going ahead, discerning God's will for the nation, discovering and showing the way towards God's kingdom. This role is to be with the people, particularly with the "least of these", not as a political party, rather, offering care and building bridges for communication, dialogue and reconciliation. This is a "treasure in clay" (2Co. 4:7), the utopia of the gospel, it is what the churches bring to the Cuban society in order to seek transformative justice and to build communities.

In this context, I would also like to mention a concrete example, i.e. our Theological Evangelical Seminary in Matanzas, which was founded in 1946 and therefore, we are celebrating our 70th Anniversary this year. One of the most outstanding empowerment tools is our *Cuban School for Diakonia*, which meets five times in our campus five days each. We work in each academic year with the same group of students, most of them diakonia practitioners at their local parishes. We just graduated a group of 20 of them and 60 in total. Our main purpose is capacity building, combining theory and practice. We have come to realize that our theological seminaries should produce pastors and church leaders trained not only to preach and teach in the four walls of the sanctuaries, not only to do Bible hermeneutics, but also social hermeneutics. We are called to form at our theological seminaries, community facilitators that are able to interpret the Christian faith in the social-political-economic context and to lead the churches to carry-out God's mission in this environment.

This *Cuban School for Diakonia* is co-organized with the Martin Luther King Center in Havana and supported through human resources by the Diakonia Area of the Cuban Council of Churches. The students are selected by the local congregations of different denominations, since our Seminary is ecumenical. One of the contents of the *School* is to explore both theoretically and in practice this *Empowering Diakonia* model explained above.

6. CONCLUSION

In the flow of the church's understanding of diakonia within the WCC, it has been underlined that it reaches out to all persons, particularly the impoverished, the "least of these" (Mt. 25:40) and oppressed, to comfort them and also to confront the root causes of injustice. Because the *missio Dei* (God's mission)[15] is holistic, diakonia is also deeply interrelated with *kerygma* (proclamation of the Word), *didache* (teaching), *leitourgia* (worship) and *martyria* (witness), which lead to *koinonia* (community). *Koinonia*, beyond the narrow boundaries of the church, is the result and ultimate goal of these functions or activities, which mark the presence of the church in the world. Diakonia, therefore, is not an end in itself, but rather an instrument used by God, together with others, to build an inclusive and just community, an *oikos*, a household in which the entire creation is included, enjoying the fullness of life intended for all.[16]

Kjell Nordstokke, in line with the arguments expressed above, reaffirms this emphasis on the community, when he stresses, "Empowerment is a process of establishing meaningful relationships. Its goal is not self-realization, as autonomous rational beings, but self-esteem activated and energized in dignified relations with others".[17] Therefore, this cross-fertilizing relationship between empowerment and diakonia seeks this ultimate goal of creating an inclusive community.

The building of this inclusive and just community is a responsibility of all humankind; where the churches have a leading role to play in this diaconal effort. As Rodolfo Gaede Neto puts it, "Diakonia is the service rendered by those who follow Jesus Christ in the perspective of the *via crucis* discipleship, being therefore an attitude of faith. It is the service provided to assist persons

---

15   David Bosch, points out that it was in the 1952 Willingen Conference of the International Mission Council where the idea (not the exact term) *missio Dei* surfaced clearly. "Mission was understood as being derived from the very nature of God", he stressed - David Bosch, *Transforming Mission. Paradigm Shifts in Theology of Mission*, 16th. edn (New York: Orbis Books, 2001), p. 587.

16   This thought is based on the report of the WCC general secretary at the time, Philip A. Potter, to its 6th Assembly, held in Vancouver, Canada, in 1983. He said: "The ecumenical movement is, therefore, the means by which the churches which form the house, the *oikos* of God, are seeking so to live and witness before all peoples that the whole *oikoumene* may become the *oikos* of God through the crucified and risen Christ in the power of the life-giving Spirit" - David Gill, *Gathered for Life. Official Report, VI Assembly of the WCC, Vancouver, Canada, 1983* (Geneva, 1983), p. 197.

17   Kjell Nordstokke, "Empowerment in the Perspective of Ecumenical Diakonia," *Diaconia*, 3 (2) (2012), p. 124.

in situations of suffering as a consequence of the exercise of oppressive power of some people over others. It is the service with a clear prophetic dimension, pointing to the denouncing and the transformation of unjust situations".[18] In this same line of thought, he goes on to say, "diakonia is defined as the renunciation of power over the people, as a denial of that power. It is the confession of the unique power of God. It is the manifestation of obedience only to the will of God. Therefore, diakonia denies hierarchy and affirms the power-service".[19]

Precisely this binomial *power-service* is a very accurate way of defining the *Empowering Diakonia* model, seeking to enable a power to serve and at the same time a service to empower that the church achieves through "an attitude of faith", i.e. a *spirituality of transformation* that embraces the *via crucis* discipleship. The model particularly enables the people from the margins to resist and overcome impoverishment, to become protagonists and to participate actively in the building of a just and inclusive world community.

7. BIBLIOGRAPHY

van Beek, Hubert, *Sharing Life in a World Community. Official Report of the WCC World Consultation on Koinonia, El Escorial, Spain, 1987* (Geneva: WCC Publications, 1989)

Bosch, David, *Transforming Mission. Paradigm Shifts in Theology of Mission*, 16th. edn (New York: Orbis Books, 2001)

Gaede Neto, Rodolfo, *La Diaconía de Jesús. Aporte Para La Fundamentación Teológica de La Diaconía En América Latina* (Buenos Aires, Argentina: Oficina Conjunta de Proyectos. Iglesia Evangélica Luterana Unida, 2005)

Gill, David, *Gathered for Life. Official Report, VI Assembly of the WCC, Vancouver, Canada, 1983* (Geneva, 1983)

---

18 Rodolfo Gaede Neto, *La Diaconía de Jesús. Aporte Para La Fundamentación Teológica de La Diaconía En América Latina* (Buenos Aires, Argentina: Oficina Conjunta de Proyectos. Iglesia Evangélica Luterana Unida, 2005), p. 187.

19 Neto, p. 183.

Ham, Carlos, *Empowering Diakonia: A Model for Service and Transformation in the Ecumenical Movement and Local Congregations*, PhD Thesis - Free University of Amsterdam (Amsterdam, Netherlands, 2015)

Ham, Carlos, 'Historical Review of the Sharing of Resources Within the Ecumenical Movement. Presented at the International Consultation on the Relationship Between Churches and Specialized Ministries / 4–10 September 2014, Nkopoloa Lodge, Malawi.' (Not published)

Kim, Dong-sung, 'Partnership and Resource Sharing', *Ecumenical Missiology. Changing Landscapes and New Conceptions of Mission*, 35 (2016), 259–70

Nordstokke, Kjell, 'Empowerment in the Perspective of Ecumenical Diakonia', *Diaconia*, 3 (2012), 185–95

Poser, Klaus, *Diakonia 2000 – Called to Be Neighbors. Official Report of the WCC World Consultation on Inter-Church Aid, Refugee and World Service, Larnaca, Cyprus, November 1986* (Geneva: World Council of Churches, 1987)

WCC, *Diakonia: Creating Harmony, Seeking Justice and Practising Compassion*, ed. by Diakonia and Solidarity Team (Geneva, 2005)

WCC, *Final Statement of Seminar on Empowerment for Diakonia in Central America and the Spanish-Speaking Caribbean, Matanzas, Cuba - 15-20 July 2012* (Matanzas, Cuba, 2012)

White, Teresa Joan, 'Diakonia', in *Dictionary of the Ecumenical Movement*, ed. by Nicholas Lossky et al, 2nd. edn (Geneva, Switzerland: WCC Publications, 2002) <www.oikoumene.org>

APPENDIX

About Korean Diakonia
http://en.koreandiakonia.org

Ever since the early days of Christian mission, Korean church has embraced the people with love of Christ by building hospitals, schools, orphanages and nursing homes. Korean Diakonia (KD) is an ecumenical organization that inherits this spirit of sharing.

Korean Diakonia is a Christian organization, composed hundreds of individual churches representing fifteen major denominations in the Republic of Korea, for example, the Presbyterian, Methodist, Baptist, Anglican, Evangelical, Pentecostal, and Holiness churches. The primary focus of the activities undertaken by KD is in the field of Christian Diakonia, service in society responding to the needs of communities with love and compassion.

Korean Diakonia intends to confirm that the Korean church stands firmly as the hope of the Korean society under the banner of "Uniting by serving & Serving as a united being", by consolidating services carried out by the local churches and individual denominations.

Korean Diakonia was established in 2007 to function as an umbrella organization that would contribute to strengthening the diaconal initiatives of the Korean churches that had thus far been conducted individual by local churches or denominations. At present KD has two distinctive entities under its structure. One is the Korean Council of Christian Social Welfare with primary focus for undertaking work in diaconal activities within the Korean peninsula, including North and South. The second entity, World Diakonia, is with responsibility for coordinating the diaconal activities globally.

The Korean Council of Christian Social Welfare was registered as a legal entity with the Ministry of Health and Welfare of the Republic of Korea in 2002 and World Diakonia was registered with the Ministry of Foreign Affairs and Trade of the Republic of Korea in 2012.

MAIN ACTIVITIES IN SOUTH KOREA

PROJECT OF SHARING WITH THE ALIENATED GROUPS WITHIN KOREA

The Korean Diakonia (KD) is progressing with the project of spending time together with the alienated neighbors during the holiday seasons (New year's day, Easter, Thanksgiving day and the Christmas), and ministries of caring for neighbors of the doss house who reside in a tiny space of 3.3058 square meter, patients with rare incurable illnesses and elderly women who are the victims of comfort women as well as the 2nd generation victims suffering from the effects of the atomic bomb. Through this, KD is assured that those people who need the accompany of the churches are not forgotten and leading in sharing the love.

DOMESTIC DISASTER RELIEF PROJECT

Since its establishment in 2007, the Korean Diakonia is working along together with the victims of the Nonhyeong-Dong boarding house incident, Yongsan incident, disaster recovery of torrential rainfall on the metropolitan area, Gumi hydrofluoric acid gas incident and the Sewol ferry tragedy, and are progressing comprehensive support project by joining together with the related organizations.

CENTER FOR VOLUNTEER

The center for volunteer of Korean Diakonia is an organization that supports Korean churches to be able to serve and perform services to the community through volunteer works from the experiences and the potential of Korean churches with its 170,000 members(parishioners) who have participated as volunteers for the clean-up work of Tae-an oil spill in 2007. The Korean Diakonia's center for volunteers are actively performing duties of jointly responding to disasters and community services by banding together with the Korea Religious Network of Volunteers(KRNV), Volunteering Korea(VKOREA) and the Korea Volunteer Center.

MAIN ACTIVITIES OVERSEAS

FOREIGN DISASTER RELIEF PROJECT

The Korean Diakonia has established corporation 'World Diakonia' and has worked on emergency relief projects from the scene of the foreign disaster areas. The emergency relief of Myanmar and China in 2008, emergency relief and the medical service for the typhoon 'Ketsana' of Philippine in 2009, emergency relief for the earthquake of Indonesia, Haiti's earthquake disaster emergency relief in 2010, emergency relief of Japan's tsunami, relief support for the 2013 Syria refugee, relief activities of 2014 Palestine Gaza-Jordan Amman, emergency relief of Nepal's earthquake disaster of 2015 and the 2016 emergency relief of earthquake disaster in Ecuador, and KD is proceeding with the projects for the residents in restoring and relieving the affected areas which may have been caused by natural disaster or man-made disaster.

FOREIGN DEVELOPMENT COOPERATION PROJECT

The World Diakonia is progressing with mid/long term projects for the foreign victims who have lost their loved ones and a place to live due to various disasters. It is giving the gift of hopes of future where the hope seems asleep, with the establishment of school in Philippine in year 2014 and establishing of Haiti's vocational school in 2016. And it is also proceeding with projects to fight against hunger in every corner of the globe.

DIAKONIA KOREA EXPO

Through hosting 'Diakonia Korea Expo 2016', following the 'Christian Social Welfare Expo 2005' and 'Christian Social Welfare Expo 2010', estimating the total volume of social serving and sharing of Korean churches, and strengthening the social problem resolving capability of Korean churches through joint cooperation of domestic and foreign relevant facilities, civil society along with central local government, it contributes in formation of great social and national consensus regarding the positive roles of Korean churches.

MAIN ACTIVITIES IN NORTH KOREA

IMPROVING NUTRITION SECURITY OF CHILDREN AND WOMEN IN NORTH KOREA

According to the result of a survey conducted in 2012 by the U.N. organization and the Bureau of Statistics of North Korea on the nutritional conditions of North Korean children and women, it was shown that 15.2% of the children under the age of 5 are underweight, 27.9% suffer from chronic malnutrition, 4% exhibit conditions of acute malnutrition and malnutrition is main in the death of children under the age of 5. And for the pregnant women, 31.2% show the symptom of anemia and a serious deficiency in complex nutrients due to leaning towards specific food groups. The nutrition support project for pregnant women and children of North Korea has considered the importance of nutrition during the 1000 days, starting from the day of pregnancy up until 2 years old, and it has provided grain powder, milk powder and nutrient enriched biscuit, and a combination of nutrient enriched powder for the vulnerable group of pregnant women and the infants in the area of North Korea.

CENTER FOR INTER-KOREAN COOPERATION

Korean Diakonia is advancing the project with the cooperation of domestic and foreign groups as well as international organizations relating to nutrition support for the pregnant mothers and children of North Korea. And project to aid the residents in the occurrence of disaster. With the establishing of the Center for Inter-Korean Cooperation. Starting in 2016, Korean Diakonia is cooperating as a partner NGO of U.N. World Food Program(WFP).